AMERICA'S
BEAUTIFUL NATIONAL PARKS

Aaron J. McKeon

AMERICA'S BEAUTIFUL NATIONAL PARKS
A Handbook for Collecting the New National Park Quarters

www.whitman**books**.com

© 2011 Whitman Publishing, LLC
3101 Clairmont Rd • Suite G • Atlanta, GA 30329

Correspondence concerning this book may be directed to the publisher, Attn: National Parks, at the address above.

ISBN: 0794828892
Printed in the United States of America

If you enjoy *America's Beautiful National Parks: A Handbook for Collecting the New National Park Quarters*, you'll also enjoy *A Guide Book of United States Coins*, popularly known as the Red Book (Yeoman, edited by Bressett); *America's Money, America's Story* (Doty); *A Guide Book of Washington and State Quarters* (Bowers); and *100 Greatest U.S. Coins* (Garrett and Guth). Related books for young collectors include *Adventure Across the States: Collecting State Quarters and Other Coins* and *Adventure Across the National Parks: Collecting National Park Quarters and Other Coins*.

WHITMAN®

For a complete catalog of hobby reference books, supplies, and storage/display products, visit Whitman Publishing online at www.whitmanbooks.com, or scan the QR code at left.

Contents

Foreword

I feel fortunate to live less than two miles from the spot in Colorado Springs where Katharine Lee Bates wrote the words to her enduring song "America the Beautiful." Miss Bates was inspired by the beauty of the area when she visited here in 1893, much as we continue to be today. I never fail to contemplate the surrounding mountains and abundant fauna and flora as I take my daily walk through the neighborhood. Being this close to our country's natural splendor is a delight for both body and soul.

People often fail to appreciate how privileged they are to live in a country that has been blessed with natural beauty literally from sea to shining sea. In a hurried world, it is seldom possible to visit the many spots of interest that are most famous for their magnificence or unique features. Many such places exist nearly forgotten by all but a fortunate few who have the chance to discover the attraction of sites they may encounter while vacationing. It is for these reasons that our American quarter-dollar coins now contain reminder-images and messages about the national parks and other stunning attractions that are accessible to all throughout the country.

Beginning in 2010, 56 of the most noteworthy attractions in the nation are being honored with special commemorative designs on the reverse of the circulating quarter-dollar coins. Points of interest include such well-known attractions as Hot Springs National Park in Arkansas, Mt. Hood National Forest in Oregon, Yellowstone National Park in Wyoming, Yosemite National Park in California, Grand Canyon National Park in Arizona, and the White Mountain National Forest in New Hampshire. Each year five different sites are selected to be depicted on their special quarter. The designs are being issued sequentially each year from 2010 to 2021, in the order in which the featured locale was established as a national park or site.

These special quarters will honor some of the most revered, historic, and beautiful places of interest throughout the United States and its territories. The designs are carefully selected to inspire interest in our nation's parks, forests, and fish and wildlife refuges, as well as to instill pride and educate the public about their importance to us and to our nation's history. Viewing a collection of these coins is like taking a mini-vacation to places we may otherwise never get to see or appreciate.

The America the Beautiful Quarters™ Program is a continuation of the immensely successful series of quarter-dollar coins that were made from 1999 through 2009 to pay tribute to each of the 50 states, the District of Columbia, and the U.S. territories of Puerto Rico, Guam, American Samoa, the U.S. Virgin Islands, and the Northern Mariana Islands. Sets of those coins have been collected by millions of Americans, and are now popular keepsakes all over the world, just as this new series of coins is destined to become.

The practice of making coins with symbolic designs began in ancient times, when sovereigns marked their money with symbols and images that could be easily understood by everyone who used them. In an age before any of the modern types of communication, coins circulated widely and were a means of spreading messages and images throughout the land. New emperors were always keen to show their portraits, and news of battles or other important information, to everyone—and coins were the quickest way to do so. The tradition has been carried on in one form or another ever since, in numerous countries. Special U.S. commemorative coins have been made since 1892. In recent years, several innovative coinage programs have been introduced to be educational, instructive, and works of art. Current issues include an annual series of dollar coins depicting each of the presidents from George Washington to the present, and companion $10 gold coins showing their spouses. Other new dollar coins have designs honoring Native Americans and their place in history and the development of the country.

Each of the 56 different "National Park" designs will eventually be placed in circulation, and with perseverance may be found in your pocket change. HAPPY HUNTING!

Kenneth Bressett
Colorado Springs, Colorado

Most American coin collectors know Kenneth Bressett as the longtime editor of the Guide Book of United States Coins—*popularly known as the "Red Book"—the best-selling coin reference guide ever published, with more than 22 million copies in print since the first edition debuted in 1946. Readers also know him as the author or editor of dozens of articles as well as other books, including* Milestone Coins: A Pageant of the World's Most Significant and Popular Money, *and the award-winning* Money of the Bible. *Bressett is a past governor, vice president, and president of the American Numismatic Association. As a former consultant to the United States Mint, he was instrumental in originating the 50 State Quarters® Program and in selecting many of the coins' reverse designs.*

Coins have been around for nearly 3,000 years, making coin collecting one of the oldest hobbies in the world. Today, there are as many as 100 million coin collectors in the United States alone. Many of them started in the hobby by collecting state quarters struck by the U.S. Mint from 1999 to 2008, and then the District of Columbia and U.S. territories quarters struck in 2009.

From 2010 through 2021, Americans are enjoying a new coinage program—one that honors national parks and sites in each of the 50 states, plus our five territories and the District of Columbia.

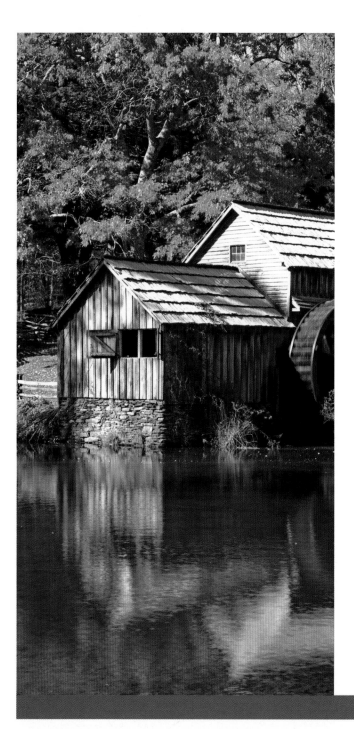

This exciting new quarter-dollar series promises to be as popular as the state quarters program that introduced millions of Americans to the joys of coin collecting.

Across the country, interest in our national parks is on the rise. The National Park Service announced that in the first six months of 2009, our parks had 4.5 million more visits than in the same period the year before. More Americans are choosing to use vacations and long weekends to visit parks in their home states (and beyond) . . . PBS has broadcast a six-episode documentary, by world-famous filmmaker Ken Burns, called "The National Parks: America's Best Idea" . . . and President Barack Obama and the first family visited Yellowstone and the Grand Canyon specifically to draw attention to the National Parks System.

America's Beautiful National Parks: A Handbook for Collecting the New National Park Quarters was designed and written for coin collectors and for everyone interested in the great outdoors. While you marvel at its awe-inspiring panoramic photographs, you will also read engaging text about each national park honored in the new coin series.

Breathtaking national parks, and an important new coinage series—two fascinating ways to learn about our great nation, all in one book. We hope you enjoy *America's Beautiful National Parks: A Handbook for Collecting the New National Park Quarters.*

Whitman Publishing
Atlanta, Georgia

For ideas on albums, folders, maps, snaplock cases, and other ways to store and display your National Park quarters, visit Whitman Publishing online at www.whitmanbooks.com. Get in touch with us by Twitter and Facebook at WhitmanCoin.

The tendency nowadays to wander in wildernesses is delightful to see. Thousands of tired, nerve-shaken, over-civilized people are beginning to find out that going to the mountains is going home; that wildness is a necessity; and that mountain parks and reservations are useful not only as fountains of timber and irrigating rivers, but as fountains of life.

—John Muir, *Our National Parks*, 1901

The ten-year-old who digs through his parents' pocket change, finds a quarter, and slides it into its spot in a Whitman coin folder gets what every experienced numismatist wants: that jolt of satisfaction at having tracked down something elusive. From 1999 through 2008, the U.S. Mint's 50 State Quarters® Program created a year-round scavenger hunt for kids and adults alike, making every fistful of change another little thicket in which the hunted quarry might be hidden. The fun continued in 2009, with quarters honoring the District of Columbia and five U.S. territories. Each unique coin honored the state, district, or territory it represented. A collection of all 56 coins offers a fascinating view of the nation.

In this way, the state quarters program, the D.C./territories quarters program, and the new America the Beautiful Quarters™ program create an entrance into the world of numismatics for the casual "loose change" collector. Most people who fill a coin folder, album, or map with quarters will not explore deep in the interior of that world; terms like *Mint State* and *obverse* will not enter their everyday language. But many who would not have looked twice at their pocket change will become interested in coin collecting because of the U.S. Mint's programs. They will be hooked by the history, artistry, culture, and friendships that the hobby offers.

The national park quarters pick up the story told by the state quarters, and carry it forward. A park, monument, or other national site will be represented for every state,

district, and territory of the United States. In some cases, these sites are the titans of the American psychological landscape: Yellowstone, Yosemite, and the Grand Canyon are just three examples. In other cases the parks may be unfamiliar, and when they turn up in this collection they'll offer chances to learn about something completely new.

Like the coinage program itself, the national parks are a sort of beachhead into an unfamiliar world. In the most practical terms, each park property provides a chance to stop your car or get off a bus, walk into a comfortable visitor's center, and talk to someone knowledgeable before diving into a place or a period in history you may know nothing

Did You Know?

They're not all parks: The official title of the new coinage series is the United States Mint America the Beautiful Quarters™ Program. The popular nickname for the coins is "national park quarters," but not all of the sites honored are *national parks*—the program also includes other kinds of national sites, such as recreation areas, national forests, memorials, monuments, shrines, parkways, wildlife refuges, scenic riverways, lakeshores, and seashores.

Pictured: Frederick Douglass National Historical Site, Washington, District of Columbia.

about. Better still, it might be a place or a period that you know a great deal about but have never *experienced*. In addition to interpreting the science behind Old Faithful into something the layman can understand, the National Park Service has protected and preserved the land and its history. The Grand Canyon you wanted to see in your youth is still there—and will be for generations to come.

HISTORY OF THE PARKS

Before 1832, no country in the world had nationally protected parks. In England, for example, Stonehenge was

John Muir (1838–1914) was born in Scotland, and his family moved to Wisconsin in 1849. Muir was a hugely influential naturalist, a writer, an early advocate of preserving the American wilderness, and the founder of the Sierra Club. Through activism he helped save the Yosemite Valley, Sequoia National Park, and other wild areas.

available for sale at private auction as recently as 1915. In the United States private owners controlled access to the Niagara River and used it and Niagara Falls for industrial purposes. Private property owners in some cases constructed walls to prevent the falls from being visible, and charged tourists to look at them through windows.

The story of the shift in values away from exploitation of resources toward their preservation and conservation is not the story of a single man or woman, a single year, a single campaign, or a single park. The National Park System was not meticulously planned: after Yellowstone National Park was created, people in different parts of the country, primarily but not exclusively in the West, argued for conservation of the treasures that they knew and loved. Conservationists

Muir and his legacy were honored on California's 2005 state quarter, designed by artist Garrett Burke.

John Muir (left) and John Burroughs: two famous defenders of America's natural resources (on Burroughs's 75th birthday, 1912).

sprang up in Louisiana and Illinois, in California and Montana. They were united by an impulse to preserve certain places: to pluck them out of the endless cycle of development and demolition and keep them as they are.

The National Park System preserves the history of the land, not just of the United States. It includes amazing geologic formations, fossils, artifacts from ancient civilizations, landmarks from the years of Spanish and French settlement, Native American lands, and the stories of island cultures in the South Pacific and Caribbean. The park system is a credit to the nation's ability to preserve more than the high points of its own story: a burial ground for slaves

is preserved, as are the Trail of Tears, a Japanese internment camp, and sites commemorating the struggle for civil rights in the 1950s and '60s.

"THE BEST IDEA WE EVER HAD"

Wallace Stegner, an environmentalist and the "Dean of Western Writers," called America's national parks "the best idea we ever had. Absolutely American, absolutely democratic, they reflect us at our best rather than our worst."

Naturalist and popular essayist John Burroughs (1837–1921) is seen here in a circa-1901 portrait entitled "Noon Meditations at Slabsides." This was Burroughs's log-cabin retreat near his home in West Park, New York. Here he grew large gardens, wrote, and received visitors such as Theodore Roosevelt, Henry Ford, and college students from nearby Vassar.

Biographers at the Library of Congress's American Memory project have ranked John Burroughs with Henry David Thoreau as one of the most important craftsmen of the American nature essay. Burroughs is an influential figure in the conservation movement.

Slabsides as it appeared in the early 21st century.

The National Park Service, in "Evolution of an Idea," describes the development of this quintessentially American concept:

Starting in the 1800s, the scenic natural wonders of the West, places like mineral springs in Arkansas, towering mountains and majestic trees of Yosemite, spouting geysers of Yellowstone, and the arid ruins of Casa Grande, inspired individual Americans to call for their preservation, asking their government to create something called "national parks."

In 1916, the work of caring for these places was moved to a new agency created by Congress for that specific

purpose. The National Park Service was given the responsibility to not only conserve and protect parks, but also to leave them "unimpaired for the enjoyment of future generations."

The job got bigger as the number and types of parks expanded. In the 1930s, military parks and national monuments were added. Then came national parkways and seashores followed by urban parks in the 1960s. During the next decade, the size of the National Park System nearly doubled with the addition of 47 million acres in Alaska.

Today numbering close to 400, national parks now include places that commemorate more recent—and in many cases more sobering—history. The stories of the fight for civil rights, the World War II Japanese American internment camps, and Sand Creek, the site of the tragic Indian massacre in 1864, are all told in national parks.

Over the years, the work of the National Park Service has moved beyond park borders. We are honored to be invited into America's communities to help build trails and playgrounds, return historic buildings to productive use, revitalize neighborhoods, expand affordable housing, protect watersheds, recognize and promote local history, and introduce the next generation to stewardship opportunities and responsibilities.

America's Best Idea just keeps getting better.

RANGER NATURALIST SERVICE
NATURE WALKS
FIELD TRIPS
CAMP FIRE-
PROGRAMS
NATURE TALKS

YELLOWSTONE
NATIONAL PARK
U.S. DEPARTMENT
OF THE INTERIOR
NATIONAL PARK
SERVICE

THE NATIONAL PARK SERVICE BY THE NUMBERS

Cumulative as of the end of fiscal year 2008:

48,000,000,000	$ incentivized in private historic preservation investment
11,700,000,000	visitors
5,409,252,508	$ in preservation and outdoor recreation grants awarded
2,750,000,000	$ annual budget
121,603,193	objects in museum collections
97,417,260	volunteer hours
84,000,000	acres of land
4,502,644	acres of oceans, lakes, and reservoirs
2,482,104	volunteers
218,000	jobs supported in gateway communities
85,049	miles of perennial rivers and streams
68,561	archeological sites
43,162	miles of shoreline
28,000	employees
27,000	historic structures
2,461	national historic landmarks
582	national natural landmarks
400	endangered species
391	national parks
40	national heritage areas
1	mission: The National Park Service cares for special places saved by the American people so that all may experience our heritage.

President Theodore Roosevelt and John Muir at Yosemite, 1903. While hiking and camping in the back country, the famous naturalist convinced the president that federal management was necessary to protect the region.

Theodore Roosevelt complained of the "tangled chaos" of North Dakota's badlands when he tried, as a young rancher, to tame his own personal portion of the West. Yet he would later proclaim that it was his time in that wilderness that gave him the fortitude to become president. (1920 copper plaque by James Earle Fraser)

THE U.S. FOREST SERVICE

Not every site honored in the America the Beautiful Quarters™ program is maintained by the National Park Service. Some are protected and managed by the U.S. Forest Service, an agency of the U.S. Department of Agriculture.

The agency was established in 1905, and its first chief, Gifford Pinchot, described its mission as "to provide the greatest amount of good for the greatest amount of people in the long run." Today the U.S. Forest Service manages 139 million acres of national forests and grasslands—an area the size of the state of Texas.

Pictured: El Yunque National Forest, Puerto Rico.

THE U.S. FISH AND WILDLIFE SERVICE

Another agency that maintains sites honored in the new coinage program is the U.S. Fish and Wildlife Service, a bureau within the Department of the Interior. Its mission is "to work with others to conserve, protect, and enhance fish, wildlife, and plants and their habitats for the continuing benefit of the American people." The agency was created in 1940.

The Fish and Wildlife Service manages 93 million acres in the National Wildlife Refuge System. This includes more than 520 national wildlife refuges and thousands of small wetlands and other special management areas. Its fisheries program operates 69 national fish hatcheries, 64 fishery resource offices, and 78 ecological services field stations.

HOT SPRINGS NATIONAL PARK

The history of Hot Springs National Park is a microcosm of the park system's history. From its earliest, contested, beginnings in 1832, it has been a site where something wonderful literally bubbles up from the natural world and interacts with the manmade. At times this has, arguably, meant the diminishment of the hot springs. In the case of the park's recent past, however, it has meant complementary development standing as an attraction in itself.

Strolling under the dogwood blossoms along Bathhouse Row in Arkansas' Hot Springs National Park, one almost forgets that it wasn't always the superb architecture of the bath houses that drew attention to this area. Originally, it was the marvel of natural hot springs that attracted visitors, who hoped that the mineral-rich waters would cure their ailments or ease chronic aches.

The value of the hot springs was clear early in the 1800s. The first official American expedition to this area was commissioned in 1804 by President Thomas Jefferson, who was eager to learn more about the southern portion of the newly acquired Louisiana Purchase. The Dunbar-Hunter Expedition, as it was known, returned with details, including news of the presence of a small cabin used by people bathing in the springs.

By the 1830s, there was sufficient concern over the possibility of destructive development near the springs that local residents successfully lobbied for federal protection of the area. President Andrew Jackson approved the creation of Hot Springs National Park in 1832. It was the first federally protected park in the nation. This protection was diluted, however, by the presence of competing property claims fought over in the courts until the 1870s. As a result, construction of private bathhouses continued through most of the 19th century.

Most of the structures built prior to the park's official re-designation in 1878 were destroyed by a fire that same year. This led to the construction of the grand architecture that makes up Bathhouse Row as it has been preserved to date.

HOT SPRINGS NATIONAL PARK

April 20, 1832 • National Park Service

YELLOWSTONE NATIONAL PARK

The Grand Prismatic Spring may be the most visually arresting sight in Yellowstone National Park. Pigmented bacteria living in a hot spring turn the edges of its pool a volcanic red-orange, shifting to yellow and yellow-green. The water in the pool's center is a sapphire blue. The vibrant colors both contrast and complement one another, unlike anything else found in nature. One of the early tourist publications on the park described it as "so dazzling that the eye cannot endure it."

Grand Prismatic is just one of the 10,000 smoking, bubbling thermal features found in Yellowstone. The incredible geysers, more than 300 of them altogether, make up the majority of geysers found on the planet. The tallest in the world, Steamboat, is found here. Old Faithful is known for both its height and its predictability.

Early explorers couldn't believe what they were seeing and, when they tried to tell people back east about the sights here, no one else did either.

When prominent geologist Ferdinand Vandeveer Hayden was planning his famed 1871 expedition to Yellowstone, he made sure to bring along photographer William Henry Jackson and landscape painter Thomas Moran, to ensure a visual record.

Hayden's expedition was more meticulous in its records of the park than previous explorations had been. His report was full of details, photographs, and sketches, and was widely distributed in Washington, building support for the preservation of these natural wonders.

The legislation creating Yellowstone National Park was signed by President Ulysses S. Grant on March 1, 1872. Prior to this date, there were no national parks anywhere in the world. Yellowstone was the first park in the world to be managed by the federal government for both the general public's enjoyment and the preservation of the park's resources. The idea was revolutionary and caught on quickly, both in the United States and around the world.

Yellowstone is a national treasure, the crown jewel in the treasure chest of the parks system. And the landscape is only part of Yellowstone's story: the wildlife habitat preserved on its 2.2 million acres is superb and means that visitors frequently get a look at large mammals like wolves, bison, elk, and bears.

More than three million people a year make the journey to northeastern Wyoming. Some hop off a tour bus, get their picture in front of Old Faithful, and hop right back on. Backcountry hikers come for long excursions into the wilderness on the park's 1,100 miles of trail. One of the easier day hikes is the five-mile Fairy Falls Trail that provides views of Fairy Falls and excellent views of Grand Prismatic Spring.

YELLOWSTONE NATIONAL PARK

March 1, 1872 • National Park Service

YOSEMITE NATIONAL PARK

Entering the Yosemite Valley in the winter is like getting into Disneyland after hours. The Douglas firs flanking the roads are draped in thick, silencing snow. The crowds that flock to the park from all parts of the globe in the summer months are absent. There are no climbers ascending the sheer face of El Capitan. Majestic Bridalveil Fall is a glittering curtain of ice. Skaters collect on a pond near the Visitor's Center and try to keep their balance while ogling Half Dome. The fireplaces are stoked in the lobby at the luxurious Ahwahnee Hotel. Nearby mountain passes may be closed, and the descent into the valley may be icy, but there is a warmth that comes from sharing these landmarks with a much smaller crowd than would be possible in the summer.

Of the millions of people who have hiked Yosemite in all seasons, one of the earliest to appreciate it was John Muir, the Scottish-born naturalist who left a prosperous career as a mechanical engineer to wander America's woods and wilds. When Muir entered the Yosemite Valley in 1868, he was smitten. He described the valley in his 1912 book, *The Yosemite:*

> It is about seven miles long, half a mile to a mile wide, and nearly a mile deep in the solid granite flank of the range. The walls are made up of rocks, mountains in size, partly separated from each other by side cañons, and they are so sheer in front, and so compactly and harmoniously arranged on a level floor, that the Valley, comprehensively seen, looks like an immense hall or temple lighted from above.

Muir wasn't the first Euro-American to enter the valley or recognize its worth. James Hutchings had brought tourists there in 1855; he became one of its early settlers and wrote a lengthy book about the area. In 1864, President Abraham Lincoln had turned the Yosemite Valley and the giant redwoods in nearby Mariposa Grove over to the state of California for their preservation.

In his explorations of the area, John Muir became convinced that more of the land around the valley needed to be preserved. His vivid descriptions of the area and the damage being done to it ultimately lead to the creation of Yosemite National Park in 1890.

Yosemite draws 3.5 million or more visitors annually, making it one of the busiest parks in the National Park System; hence the appeal of at least one visit in the winter. Many visitors come to see the landmarks immortalized in Ansel Adams's exquisite black-and-white photographs of the park.

YOSEMITE NATIONAL PARK

October 1, 1890 • National Park Service

GRAND CANYON NATIONAL PARK

Robert B. Stanton was the chief engineer on an 1889 expedition to the Grand Canyon. Later he wrote: "It is impossible in a few pages to do justice, in the smallest degree, to the great gorge itself—that sublimest thing on earth. . . . What then shall we write?"

As Stanton fretted, mere words are inadequate to describe the primal beauty of this iconic American landmark. The canyon has an average depth of 4,000 feet. Over this gorge cut by the Colorado River soar cliffs whose colors defy description. They are red and white and pink and dotted with green brush, and they change with each subtle variance in the light. Painters have been more successful than writers in conveying the Grand Canyon's beauty to those who have never seen it up close. Some of the earliest American visitors to the canyon were landscape artists, including Frederick Dellenbaugh and Thomas Moran, who accompanied John Wesley Powell on expeditions in the 1870s.

The land the park occupies has been in continuous human use for tens of thousands of years. It has been occupied by the Anasazi, the Cohonina, the Paiutes, the Cerbat, and the Navajo. The canyon has been a tourist destination since the late 19th century. Visitors arrived first by stagecoach, then by train, and later by automobile. By 1905 a luxury hotel was available for guests. By 1919, more than 40,000 tourists visited each year.

Thomas Moran's paintings influenced President Theodore Roosevelt to name the area a national monument in 1908, declaring the canyon "the one great sight that every American should see." It became a national park in 1919, just three years after the founding of the National Park Service.

Nearly five million tourists visit the Grand Canyon each year. Most stick to the more accessible South Rim, while a smaller number venture to the more remote North Rim or into the Inner Canyon. The canyon can be viewed from many different vantage points, including from boats on float trips along the Colorado River, by mule rides departing from both the South and North Rims, or from the historic Yavapai Observation Station. Each visitor to this great landscape leaves, no doubt, with some inkling of what Stanton felt so long ago.

MT. HOOD NATIONAL FOREST

Mt. Hood National Forest in northwestern Oregon is Portland's playground, complete with a splash park (the Clackamas River), plenty of space for picnics (124,000 acres of wilderness area), and a large climbing area. With more than a million acres of land, the forest offers 150 well-stocked lakes and ponds, whitewater rafting, skiing, hiking, snowboarding, and camping.

Located 20 miles east of Portland, it receives 4.5 million visits annually. According to the U.S. Forest Service, the average visitor comes to the forest 17 times a year, so it doesn't really see 4.5 million different people annually. It is more likely that many people in the region spend every weekend here in the summer and/or winter months.

For mountain climbers with experience in technical climbing, the 11,200-foot summit of Mt. Hood beckons. The trail to the peak begins at Timberline Lodge, which is itself worth a trip to the forest. The Timberline was constructed in the 1930s by craftsmen from the Works Progress Administration and the Civilian Conservation Corps. The privately run lodge, which is also a ski resort in the winter months, is a national historical landmark.

Hundreds of miles of trails lead hikers beneath the forest's brilliant-green fir trees and along crystal-clear streams. The longer hikes include 100 miles of the rugged Pacific Crest National Scenic Trail, running through the forest, as well as the 40-mile Timberline Trail into the Mt. Hood Wilderness. Shorter trails are no less amazing, such as the six-mile Tom, Dick, and Harry Loop, which is frequently identified as one of the best hikes in the state.

Mt. Hood National Forest is part of a much larger collection of national forests in Oregon extending along the Cascade Mountain Range from the Columbia River to California. The entire area was one huge entity, originally called the Cascade Range Forest Reserve. This reserve was created in 1893 with massive popular support from the people in the region. As the numbers suggest, this support has only grown stronger over time.

MT. HOOD NATIONAL FOREST

GETTYSBURG NATIONAL MILITARY PARK

"It is rather for us to be here dedicated to the great task remaining before us, that from these honored dead we take increased devotion to that cause for which they gave the last full measure of devotion, that we here highly resolve that these dead shall not have died in vain, that this nation, under God, shall have a new birth of freedom, and that government of the people, by the people, for the people, shall not perish from the earth."

These words, from President Abraham Lincoln's stirring Gettysburg Address, were part of the ceremony dedicating Soldiers National Cemetery in Gettysburg, Pennsylvania, on November 19, 1863. At that point, the cost in human lives of the War Between the States had gone far beyond what most would have predicted. The numbers of Americans dead and wounded in the major battles prior to Gettysburg, fought in places like Shiloh, Antietam, Fredericksburg, and Chancellorsville, dwarfed the number of casualties in all previous American wars combined.

Most historians refer to the Battle of Gettysburg as the turning point in the Civil War. It marked the Confederate Army's last major offensive and the end of General Robert E. Lee's drive to invade the Union. Gettysburg was the largest and bloodiest battle of the war, involving 170,000 soldiers and resulting in 51,000 casualties.

Gettysburg National Military Park offers an education in the hair's breadth by which history is sometimes determined. The skirmishes and battles fought in the orchards and on the hills and fields preserved here determined the course of the war and, with it, the destiny of our nation.

The monuments to the fallen of both sides are sobering, but the size and openness of the field across which Pickett's Charge took place is astonishing. The bravery and grit of the Confederate soldiers who marched across this meadow, in the face of crushing artillery and rifle fire, comes across in a way that no history book could hope to rival. Similarly, visitors get a much better sense of how the 20th Maine regiment could possibly have pulled off the defense of Little Round Top, where a potentially disastrous Confederate advance on the Union's flank was just barely averted.

The battlefield at Gettysburg is considered by many to be as close to sacred land as a battlefield could be. Visitors absorb its lessons by way of guided tours and the many interpretive materials in the Visitor's Center.

GETTYSBURG NATIONAL MILITARY PARK

February 11, 1895 • National Park Service

GLACIER NATIONAL PARK

In Glacier National Park, sapphire streams pour through narrow gorges, grizzly bears roam the valley, and rock walls and mountains spring up from the shores of pristine lakes. Glacier National Park is one of the wildest and most remote parks in the continental United States. The park is one of the best places to get to know the Rocky Mountain wilderness. There are 700 miles of hiking trails, guided horseback rides, a dozen campgrounds, and four lakes that allow boating.

The Continental Divide runs through the park, splitting the wildlife habitat in two. The park's "Mammal Checklist" clarifies which species can be found on which side of the divide. Bobcats, lynx, mountain lions, coyotes, wolves, elk, moose, bighorn sheep, and mountain goats are found on both sides. Bison and pronghorn are only found in the prairies on the eastern side of the divide.

Thanks to the Going to the Sun Road, which traverses the park east to west, visitors needn't bother too much about figuring out which side of the Divide to see first. This sometimes dizzying mountain road *can* be driven in about two hours —but given its marvelous distractions, visitors should plan on spending more than two hours here.

Glacier National Park's neighbor directly to the north is Waterton Lakes National Park in Canada. Together, the two parks form an International Peace Park.

Glacier National Park's history is interesting primarily because of what it is missing. Located in remote Montana, far from major (or even mid-sized) cities, there was little chance of this area becoming a location for 19th-century industry or private estates: it was largely inaccessible. The driving force for its dedication as a national park was the Great Northern Railway, which ran along what is now the park's southern border. Railroad executives knew that, with federal designation, the beauty of the wild and mountainous area to the north of their railway could be better promoted and would be made more accessible to the public. The Great Northern Railroad went on to build several chalets within the park. Several of them are now listed on the National Register of Historic Places.

GLACIER NATIONAL PARK

February 22, 1897 • National Park Service

OLYMPIC NATIONAL PARK

iking the 17-mile Hoh River Trail in Olympic National Park means climbing 4,400 feet, from the mossy and temperate rain forest on the western slopes of the Olympic Mountains, through a subalpine forest and on to Blue Glacier, on the shoulders of Mount Olympus. After the click of your car doors closing at the trailhead, you are alone with the sounds of the Hoh River Valley. Everything you need for the next two days is on your back. Like the earliest visitors to this area, you are hunting the majestic Roosevelt elk. Unlike those pioneers, who started showing up in the late 1800s, you are using a camera, not a rifle, and you will leave this last free-roaming herd none the worse for your visit.

The ascent to Blue Glacier is only one of hundreds of adventures beckoning visitors to Olympic National Park. Located on the remote Olympic Peninsula in western Washington State, this park is a smorgasbord of outdoor recreation. In addition to rain forest, lakes, waterfalls, glaciers, and mountain peaks, the park includes long stretches of untamed Pacific coastline. Hurricane Ridge, at 5,400 feet, is the most accessible area for day use, particularly in the winter. Skis and snowshoe rental are available—and sledding on the ridge is not as treacherous as it sounds.

The Olympic Peninsula is as far west as you can drive in the lower 48 states. To the north lies Vancouver, Canada. The area is so remote that as late as 1890 Europeans had not yet crossed the Olympic Mountain Range.

The Native Americans of the Pacific Northwest lived in this area for millennia, fishing for salmon and hunting the plentiful local game. Twelve thousand years ago, this included elephant-like mammals called *mastodons*. In 1977 a mastodon skeleton was uncovered, along with a 12,000-year-old spear point. The native peoples were reduced by diseases carried by Europeans before the Europeans themselves began moving into the Peninsula in large numbers.

U.S. Army lieutenant Joseph P. O'Neil is credited with the earliest explorations of this area, first in the summer of 1885, when his expedition ascended Hurricane Ridge and Mount Anderson, and again in the summer of 1890, when his team reached the summit of Mount Olympus.

O'Neil is also credited with the idea of creating a national park here. He wrote a report to Congress in 1896, stating that "while the country on the outer slope of these mountains is valuable, the interior is useless for all practicable purposes. It would, however, serve admirably for a national park." A year later, in 1897, President Grover Cleveland created the Olympic Forest Reserve. This designation, however, did not protect the herds of Roosevelt elk that were being hunted. In 1909, President Theodore Roosevelt created Mount Olympus National Monument within the reserve, protecting the elk. President Franklin Roosevelt visited the area in 1937 and, a year later, designated it a national park. The wild coastline area was added in 1953.

OLYMPIC NATIONAL PARK

February 22, 1897 • National Park Service

VICKSBURG NATIONAL MILITARY PARK

In 21st-century warfare, crippling an enemy's satellite communications is as important as blocking highways and ports and destroying airfields. Centuries of improvements in military technology have multiplied the means of warfare, if not the underlying strategy. One of the fundamentals continues to be interrupting the enemy's flow of information, troops, and supplies.

At the time of the American Civil War, there was no bigger highway than the Mississippi River. Prior to the war it had meant that the cotton-producing regions of the Southern states could ship goods both north and south to the port at New Orleans. The river was the economic lifeline of the nation's interior, and cities sprouted up along its shores: Minneapolis, St. Paul, Davenport, St. Louis, Memphis, Baton Rouge, New Orleans. During the Civil War, control of the river became critical to both economic power and the movement of men, artillery, and supplies.

After the capture of New Orleans by Union troops in 1862, Vicksburg became the last Confederate stronghold on the Mississippi. President Abraham Lincoln considered the capture of Vicksburg essential to the war. He called Vicksburg "the key," stating that "we can take all the northern ports of the Confederacy, and they can defy us from Vicksburg."

With the Confederacy's defenses at Vicksburg, on bluffs 200 feet above the river, the Union's naval power on the river was split in two. A naval assault in 1862 failed to take the city. A number of strategies involving the creation of canals to bypass Vicksburg were also unsuccessful. Grant's solution was to approach from the east, through swamplands considered impassable. With both naval support and reinforcements from General William T. Sherman, the eastern approach was successful and led to the capture of several smaller cities to the east of Vicksburg. Still unable to overwhelm Vicksburg's defenses, however, Grant began digging his artillery in around the city, preparing for a siege.

The siege brought constant bombardment of the city and the slow starvation of the 30,000 troops and 5,000 residents living there. This lasted for six long weeks. On July 3, Vicksburg raised the white flag and the two generals met to discuss the terms of surrender. After Union troops occupied the city, the Confederacy lost its ability to control Union activity on the Mississippi: the major north-south route for trade and military movement was in Union hands.

Vicksburg National Military Park gives visitors a window into this pivotal point in the Civil War. Topography played a crucial role in both Vicksburg's importance and in how the city was captured. The artifacts on display in the park's museum include those taken from the USS *Cairo*, a sunken gunboat dredged from the mud on the bottom of the Mississippi.

CHICKASAW NATIONAL RECREATION AREA

[The Lincoln Bridge] is not a thing apart—it is as if it had grown there and been made when the rugged banks of the stream and the trees were made.

—Albert R. Greene, 1909

When we entered the park, we lost all stress. There is nothing like the natural beauty of this place and the water. I can't mention the water enough, it is so soothing.

—Isabell Austell

Chickasaw National Recreation Area has a long history as an Indian reservation, mineral springs, and a pioneer community. It is also known for the improvements made there during the 1930s by the Civilian Conservation Corps.

The area that is now Chickasaw National Recreation Area was, for much of the 1800s, the Chickasaw district of the Indian Territory. The Chickasaw had been displaced from their ancestral lands in the Natchez Trace area, in what is now Mississippi and Alabama. The Native Americans were relocated to the arid lands in present-day Oklahoma.

As a map of the United States shows, white settlers did not stop at the Mississippi, and it was not long before settlers moved into what would become the Indian Territory. The presence of mineral springs and an oasis-like setting at the confluence of the Sulphur and Rock creeks made this part of the Chickasaw district attractive; it wasn't long before the small village of Sulphur sprouted up. By the end of the 19th century, Sulphur had 1,800 residents.

In order to clear up their rights to the land, and to protect the mineral springs in the vicinity from exploitation, the settlers pressed for the creation of a national park, along the lines of Hot Springs in Arkansas. The Chickasaw Nation agreed to the importance of protecting the natural resources, and sold 640 acres to the federal government for the creation of Sulphur Springs Reservation in 1902.

The park was renamed Platt National Park in 1906, in honor of Senator Orville Platt, who had guided the park's legislation through Congress. The name was changed again in 1976 when Platt National Park and a nearby reservoir were combined to create the 10,000-acre property now known as Chickasaw National Recreation Area.

2012 · PUERTO RICO

EL YUNQUE NATIONAL FOREST

There are more species of trees in El Yunque than in all the rest of the United States Forest System combined. . . . Among the many healing plants found in the forest are the Ortiga brava or stinging nettle (Urtica urens), *the Yagrumo hembra or weathervane tree* (Cecropia peltata), *and the tabonuco tree* (Dacryoides excelsa). *All are used in the folk medicine on the island. Puerto Rico has over 135 plants with recognized major medicinal uses and an additional 170 with minor therapeutic value. . . . Medicine has a stake in the rain forest, and El Yunque is a national treasure.*

—T.T. Martinez & R.R. Martinez, *Medicinal Herbs From the Caribbean National Forest (El Yunque), Puerto Rico*

There are surprises around every bend in the trail at El Yunque National Forest in Puerto Rico. With mountain peaks of up to 3,500 feet catching buckets of rainfall every day, El Yunque is like a jade castle rising out of the eastern hills of the island.

Established to preserve the lush vegetation and exotic species in the Loquillo Mountains, this 28,000-acre forest reserve is the only tropical rainforest in the U.S. National Forest system. The combination of a warm Caribbean climate and 12 feet of rain annually (16 feet in the mountain peaks) has created a unique ecosystem that supports more than 250 different animal species. The highly endangered Puerto Rican Amazon parrot was, for years, reduced to 30 birds found only in this forest.

To experience the "true" rain forest, visitors must hike to elevations above 2,500 feet. Here the cloud cover is virtually constant and the vegetation, subjected to perpetual wind and rain, rarely grows to be more than 15 feet tall. As a result it is sometimes referred to as a *cloud forest* or a *dwarf forest*. While pushing between giant palm fronds on the trails' lower elevations, a visitor is sure to hear the song of the tiny coqui frog and catch sight of exquisite orchids. Spending the night in the forest is the best way to get to know its unique sounds and smells, but it presents many challenges. While there are no large mammals or poisonous snakes to contend with, the omnipresent rain and lack of developed sites mean that it is not for the casual camper.

Preserving the treasures of El Yunque was considered imperative even before Puerto Rico became part of the United States. In 1876, while Puerto Rico was a Spanish property, King Alphonso XII created the Loquillo Forest, preserving the area's trees, water, and minerals and making it one of the first forest preserves in the Western hemisphere. In 1898, Puerto Rico became a U.S. commonwealth and in 1906 President Theodore Roosevelt established the Loquillo Forest Reserve, which later became El Yunque National Forest.

El Yunque National Forest • HC-01, Box 13490, Rio Grande, Puerto Rico, 00745-9625

EL YUNQUE NATIONAL FOREST

CHACO CULTURE NATIONAL HISTORICAL PARK

Our National Park System is not only a doorway into the world of nature and United States history—the doors of the park system also open on the threshold of ancient, vanished civilizations. Upon arrival at a place like Chaco Culture National Historic Park in northwestern New Mexico, the average visitor may not know anything about the Anasazi, the Ancient Ones who inhabited the American Southwest and vanished centuries before the arrival of Europeans. After visiting Chaco Canyon, even the casual visitor is bound to be left in awe at the complexity of the civilization that organized and built the city that flourished here hundreds of years ago.

The ruins in Chaco Canyon are fascinating to modern Americans because they are startlingly urban. An estimated 5,000 to 6,000 people lived in and around the canyon, using irrigation to draw water from natural pools in the surrounding cliffs, building rigidly straight roads and planning out multi-storied homes. The ruins are also compelling because they give modern Americans a picture of a complex civilization, like our own, built out of a completely different way of looking at the world. From huge, underground ceremonial chambers (known as *kivas*) to the alignment of structures to precise north-south or astronomic directions, the ruins are foreign and yet familiar.

The 14 "Great Houses" were large even by modern hotel-industry standards, ranging from 100 to 650 rooms. The purpose of the Great Houses is still mysterious, but there is speculation that this area was the center of a large system of trading and food distribution. This hypothesis is supported by the vast system of roads in the region.

An estimated 200 miles of roads connect Chaco Canyon to other settlements in the area. They are remarkable because of their straightness: they do not bend around hills or gulleys. The road system is mysterious because of its extensiveness. Modern Americans didn't realize it was there until the advent of aerial photography.

The wealth of information on ancient civilizations preserved at Chaco Canyon has led to its inclusion in the United Nations Educational, Scientific and Cultural Organization's (UNESCO) list of World Heritage sites. These are sites deemed to be of value to, and to some extent that belong to, all people, regardless of nation. Other World Heritage sites include the Pyramids of Egypt and the Great Barrier Reef.

ACADIA NATIONAL PARK

The Wabanaki Indians called the island that is today home to Acadia National Park *Pemetic:* the sloping land. Traveling the coast in 1604, French explorer Samuel de Champlain named this island Mount Desert because of its barren, rocky mountaintops. The park is known today as a place where the mountains meet the sea—there are more than 20 peaks, ranging from 280 to more than 1,500 feet. Cadillac Mountain (the highest, at 1,530 feet) may be the first part of the continental United States to see the sun each day.

Acadia National Park is made up of nearly 48,000 acres of Maine coast about three hours northeast of Portland. There are over 120 miles of trails within the park, ranging from the very easy to the nearly vertical. Precipice Trail requires the hiker to use iron rungs and ladders built into the side of Champlain Mountain.

Visitors who happen to bring their jodhpurs and an appaloosa are well positioned to take advantage of the more than 50 miles of car-free carriage roads that wind around the park. Millionaire philanthropist John D. Rockefeller Jr. designed, financed, and oversaw much of the construction of these roads, which are often cited as the finest remaining examples of their kind. (Rockefeller designed roadways in several other parks; the parkway between Yellowstone and Grand Teton National Park bears his name.) Naturally, the carriage roads are also available for carriage rides, in addition to being open to pedestrians and, in the winter, cross-country skiers.

The history of the Maine coast is rich with stories of Glooscap, the man-god of the Wabanaki, and with stories of French and British settlement of this area. In its recent history, that is to say, in the late 1800s, Mount Desert Island was a vacation spot for the very rich—the Vanderbilts, Rockefellers, Astors, Fords, and others—who had estates here. The mansions were largely destroyed in 1947 in a fire, but, prior to that, it was the area's wealthiest citizens who banded together to buy up land in the area and set it aside for public use.

Led by George B. Dorr, this group lobbied for the creation of a national park. Writing in 1913, Dorr summarized the pragmatic conservationist's impulse: "By taking thought in season, little need be sacrificed to secure incalculable benefits in Nature's wilder near-by regions, in her grander landscapes that lie within the reach of busy men; in refreshing forests, not too limited; in picturesque and open downs beside the sea; or along the pleasant, wooded side of streams with unpolluted water." The efforts of Dorr and the other members of the Hancock County Trustees of Public Reservations were rewarded when President Woodrow Wilson created Lafayette National Park in 1916. Its name was later changed to Acadia.

ACADIA NATIONAL PARK

July 8, 1916 • National Park Service

HAWAI'I VOLCANOES NATIONAL PARK

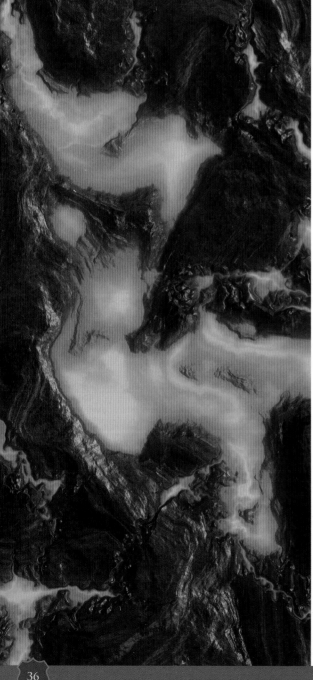

After walking some distance over the sunken plain, which in several places sounded hollow under our feet, we at length came to the edge of the great crater, where a spectacle, sublime and even appalling, presented itself before us—"We stopped and trembled." . . . Immediately before us yawned an immense gulf, in the form of a crescent, about two miles in length, from north-east to south-west, nearly a mile in width, and apparently 800 feet deep. The bottom was covered with lava, and the south-west and northern parts of it were one vast flood of burning matter, in a state of terrific ebullition, rolling to and fro its "fiery surge" and flaming billows. Fifty-one conical islands, of varied form and size, containing so many craters, rose either round the edge or from the surface of the burning lake. Twenty-two constantly emitted columns of gray smoke, or pyramids of brilliant flame; and several of these at the same time vomited from their ignited mouths streams of lava, which rolled in blazing torrents down their black indented sides into the boiling mass below.

—William Ellis, *A Journal of a Tour around Hawaii, the Largest of the Sandwich Islands* (1825)

According to legend, Pele, the volcano goddess, came to Hawaii to find a home. She used a stick to dig pits in the Hawaiian islands, but her water-goddess sister filled each of them with water. When Pele reached Mount Kilauea, on the big island, she dug deeper and her sister was unable to douse the fires. Pele's passions and jealousies produce the mountain's violent eruptions, which continue to this day.

When the English missionary the Reverend William Ellis visited Kilauea in 1823, he was warned that he was entering "Pele's dominions." He proceeded to descend into the crater, where he got a look into what he described in his journal as "one vast flood of burning matter, in a state of terrific ebullition, rolling to and fro its 'fiery surge' and flaming billows."

Exploring Hawai'i Volcanoes National Park, you are squarely on Pele's home turf. Portions of Chain of Craters Road, the main road to Kilauea's rim, is periodically closed because of active lava flows. Visitors to the area are constantly warned of new vents and of the possibility of dangerous gases being emitted. Flows of lava into the Pacific are by no means uncommon. The island of Hawaii is, literally, not done cooking.

The national park includes the summits of both Kilauea (3,980 feet above sea level) and its mightier neighbor to the north, Mauna Loa (13,600 feet above sea level). Mauna Loa is the largest volcano in the world and, measured from its beginnings at the bottom of the sea floor, has a total height of 56,000 feet. Mauna Loa has not erupted since 1984, but the U.S. Geological Survey provides constant updates on the volcano's status and activity level.

Visitors to the national park can experience Kilauea by way of an 11-mile drive around the crater's rim.

DENALI NATIONAL PARK AND PRESERVE

It's the great, big, broad land 'way up yonder,
It's the forests where silence has lease;
It's the beauty that thrills me with wonder,
It's the stillness that fills me with peace.

So run the closing lines from Robert Service's "The Spell of the Yukon." Hiking across the trackless tundra of Denali National Park, blasted by frigid winds, in a land of glaciers and grizzlies, the Alaskan wilderness is sensationally beautiful, but is obviously not to be trifled with.

The park, made up of 9,400 square miles of Alaskan wilderness, is slightly larger than the state of Vermont. Located on the Alaskan Mountain Range, about 240 miles due north of Anchorage, it is neither the largest nor the most remote of the national parks. The presence of Mount McKinley, the highest point on the North American continent (20,300 feet above sea level), makes Denali the best-known Alaskan park. It attracts mountain climbers from around the world.

The ascent of Denali is not for the casual visitor and requires extensive training and preparation. For a frame of reference: no lone climber scaled to the top of the mountain until August 1970, when Japanese explorer and adventurer Naomi Uemura did it (he was also the first explorer to reach the North Pole alone, in 1978). In February 1984 he returned to attempt the first solo ascent of McKinley in the winter. Uemura's Japanese flag was eventually found planted at the summit—but his body was never recovered.

Hiking around the park itself offers plenty of adventure. Other than a few trails near the Visitor Center on the northeastern end of the park, trails are not marked. Bus tours are offered that take visitors much farther into the park than they would be likely to get on their own: private vehicles are only allowed to access the first 14 miles of the park's road system.

Yogi Berra once said of a famous restaurant, "Nobody goes there anymore; it's too crowded." Denali does not have this problem. Because of its remoteness, Denali sees about 400,000 people annually, compared to the 3,000,000 who enter Yellowstone. While most of these visitors are sane enough to come in the summer months, you can get into isolated back-country areas fairly quickly for such a well-known park.

DENALI NATIONAL PARK AND PRESERVE

February 26, 1917 • National Park Service

WHITE MOUNTAIN NATIONAL FOREST

A wilderness, in contrast with those areas where man and his own works dominate the landscape, is hereby recognized as an area where the earth and its community of life are untrammeled by man, where man himself is a visitor who does not remain . . . retaining its primeval character and influence, without permanent improvements or human habitation, which is protected and generally appears to have been affected primarily by the forces of nature, with the imprint of man's work substantially unnoticeable . . . has outstanding opportunities for solitude or a primitive and unconfined type of recreation; . . . is of sufficient size as to make practicable its preservation and use in an unimpaired condition; and may also contain ecological, geological, or other features of scientific, educational, scenic, or historical value.

—The Wilderness Act, 1964

Fall in White Mountain National Forest in northern New Hampshire means mile after mile bursting with all of the colors of the autumnal palette. Birches, sugar maples, and stately American beeches are draped across this landscape that was, 150 years ago, largely cleared and settled by farmers. The summit of Mount Washington, at 6,300 feet, is the highest peak in New England and is the goal of climbers wishing to "bag" the many peaks of the Presidential Range that rise to more than 4,000 feet.

In addition to hiking, mountain climbing, and general "leaf peeping," the White Mountains are a popular destination for skiing, snow boarding, and mountain biking. The White Mountain National Forest sees about seven million visitors annually, making it one of the most popular places in the national park system, owing largely to its proximity to the major cities of the northeast.

The urbanization of the northeast is a big part of White Mountain National Forest's history. Settlers began arriving in the mountains in the 17th and 18th centuries. Farmers cleared and lived on the land for generations, but the terrain was relatively unproductive. By the early 1800s, farmers began abandoning the area and logging interests bought it up. Conservation groups pushed for preservation of the White Mountains, but in the early 1900s there was political resistance to federal spending to preserve scenic areas on the eastern seaboard. In 1911, the Weeks Act authorized federal spending for the conservation of land at the headwaters of major rivers. The White Mountains were among the first lands to be bought up for conservation under the act. The National Forest was established by President Woodrow Wilson in 1918.

WHITE MOUNTAIN NATIONAL FOREST

PERRY'S VICTORY AND INTERNATIONAL PEACE MEMORIAL

"Tell the men to fire faster and not to give up the ship." These were the dying words of Captain James Lawrence, commander of the USS *Chesapeake*, who was mortally wounded in a naval battle in Boston Harbor during the War of 1812. His dying words were paraphrased as "Don't give up the ship" and stitched in white on the blue field of Commander Oliver Perry's battle flag. When Perry's squadron closed with the more heavily armed British squadron near Ohio in September 1813, he hoisted this flag on the USS *Lawrence* as a sign of his defiance and determination.

The British ships were under Commander Robert Barclay, who was attempting to dislodge the American navy from Lake Erie in order to clear British supply and communication routes on the lake. His six ships were armed with cannon with twice the range of those of the nine vessels in the American squadron.

The Battle of Lake Erie was nearly a disaster for Perry. His flagship was destroyed by the barrage from the British long guns and most of his crew was either dead or wounded. Unwilling to give up, and showing supreme tenacity, he found four able-bodied sailors and his battle flag and rowed to the nearby USS *Niagara*. Commanding the more or less unscathed *Niagara*, Perry was able to reorganize his squadron and pour shot into the British ships, which had also been heavily damaged. The British surrendered and Perry wrote to Brigadier General William Henry Harrison: "We have met the enemy and they are ours."

Today, Perry's battle flag is on display at the U.S. Naval Academy at Annapolis, Maryland. The American victory, and the subsequent century of peace between the United States, Canada, and Britain, is commemorated on South Bass Island, near Ohio, in Lake Erie. Beneath the base of the 352-foot monument are interred the remains of three American and three British officers killed in the battle.

Construction of the monument began in 1912, with the purpose of celebrating peace in a world that was amassing new and stronger weapons.

GREAT BASIN NATIONAL PARK

Perfect places for star gazing are becoming rarer and rarer in the United States. Air pollution and light pollution have made it hard for a kid with a backyard telescope to spot the Milky Way and the planets of our own solar system. In order to get a good look at the night sky, you need to get away from strip malls and parking lots and you need to get into the higher elevations, where the air is clear.

Great Basin National Park, originally known for the subterranean treasures of Lehman Caves, is among the best places in the country from which to look at the night sky, because it is both far away from civilization and relatively accessible. With elevations ranging from 6,500 to 12,000 feet, it feels like there is nothing between you and the cosmos but your blanket.

Great Basin sits due south of U.S. Highway 50, often called the Loneliest Road in America. The nearest "major" city is Ely, Nevada—population 4,000. Great Basin sees many fewer visitors than other national parks that are closer to big cities. Established in 1922 by President Warren G. Harding, it was originally called Lehman Caves National Monument. Lehman Caves is a natural wonder: a limestone cavern that was so full of ancient stalactites and stalagmites, crafted by Nature's own hand over millenia, that the first party of explorers vowed to return with sledgehammers in order to break their way through the rock formations and reach other portions of the caverns.

Today, Lehman Caves is accessible only by guided tours, and most of the other 40 caves in the park are off limits. Eight caves are accessible by special permit to spelunkers who know what they're doing.

Lehman Caves became Great Basin National Park in 1986, in recognition of the other unique and amazing natural features presenting the area. These include both Mount Wheeler, the highest peak in the park, and Wheeler Peak Glacier, one of the southernmost glaciers in the United States.

Another feature not to be missed is the small groves of Bristlecone pine trees found in the park. Because the Great Basin gets a minuscule amount of rain every year, its vegetation is primarily made up of the most resourceful shrubs and scrub trees. Of these, the heartiest is doubtless the Bristlecone pine, a tree so well adapted to harsh conditions that it does not always add a new ring in a year of growth. It grows slowly and densely—so much so that, while Bristlecones are among the oldest living things, they typically grow to be less than 30 feet tall. In 1964, a researcher was given permission to remove a Bristlecone from Great Basin. The tree was called "Prometheus" and it turned out to be 4,600 years old. Giant sequoias are larger, but typically not as old.

GREAT BASIN NATIONAL PARK

FORT MCHENRY NATIONAL MONUMENT AND HISTORIC SHRINE

O say, does that star-spangled banner yet wave
O'er the land of the free and the home of the brave?

—From "The Star Spangled Banner,"
U.S. national anthem

The U.S. national anthem was born out of one man's happiness at seeing that his country's flag was still flying. The banner, still waving, was the sign that his city, his country, and his liberty had been preserved after what must have seemed like an endless and fiery attack.

The man was a lawyer from Baltimore named Francis Scott Key, and he happened to be in Baltimore Harbor on a British truce ship, rather than in his house, because he had been negotiating with the British for the release of one of their prisoners of war, an American doctor. The British agreed to release the doctor, but would not let the Americans return to Baltimore because the bombardment of Fort McHenry was commencing, and the Americans had just seen the size, strength, and position of the British ships that had come to destroy their city.

Before burning and sacking Baltimore, as they had just done to Washington a few weeks earlier, the British had to get past the defenses of Fort McHenry at the gateway to the city's Northwest Harbor on Chesapeake Bay. In the 1800s, Baltimore was known as a major international seaport and as a center of shipbuilding. Baltimore was a target for the British both because it was the third-largest city in the nation and because the port was a base of operations for privateers—non-military ships that were brought into service to supplement the young nation's relatively weak navy. There were about 185 of these licensed pirates, officially commissioned by the U.S. government to harass the British and interrupt trade wherever possible.

With the fate of Baltimore hanging in the balance, Francis Scott Key watched from the harbor as the British ships began launching rockets and cannonballs at the fort on the morning of September 13, 1814. With their ships out of range of McHenry's guns, the British could keep up the bombardment for a full day. Though they threw at the fort everything they had, estimated at 1,800 bombs and rockets, few of these actually hit their target. Because the fort was well constructed, the bombs that hit did little damage to the cannon defending Baltimore.

On the morning of the 14th, it was clear that the British naval assault had ended in a stalemate and that both fort and city had survived. The American banner still waved over the fortress, inspiring Key to write his poem "The Defence of Fort McHenry," jotting down verses while still stuck in the harbor. He set the poem to the tune of "To Anacreon in Heaven," originally written for a gentlemen's club in London. It became the U.S. national anthem in 1931.

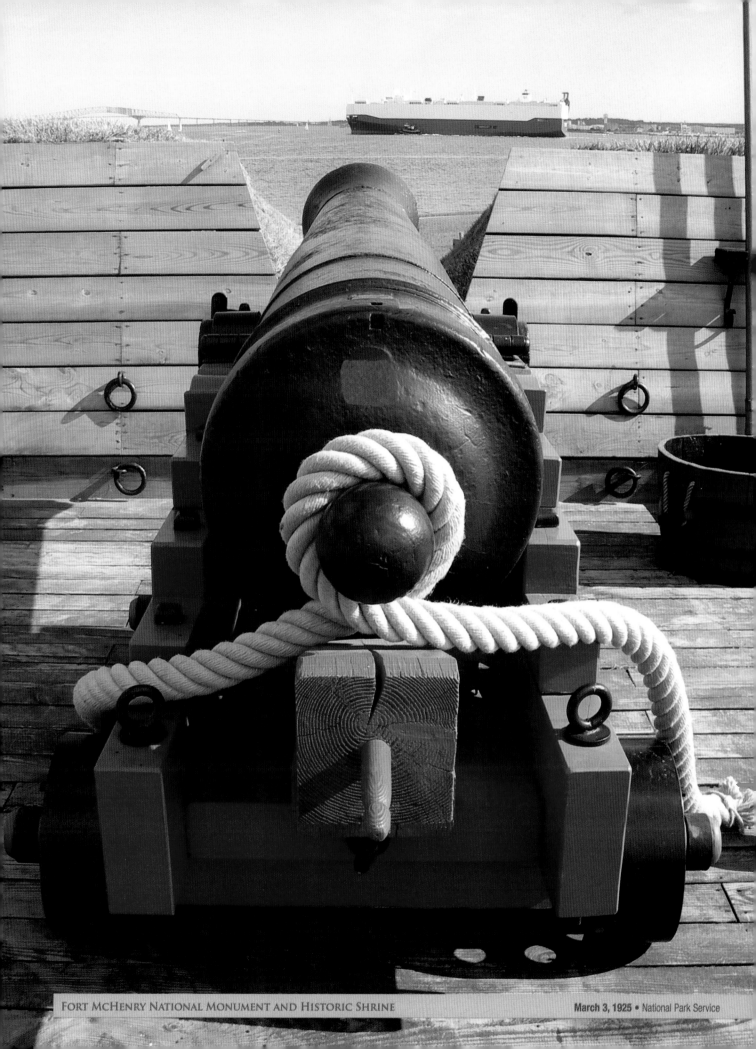

FORT McHENRY NATIONAL MONUMENT AND HISTORIC SHRINE

March 3, 1925 • National Park Service

MOUNT RUSHMORE NATIONAL MEMORIAL

When he spoke at the unveiling of the gigantic granite bust of Thomas Jefferson on Mount Rushmore in 1936, President Franklin Roosevelt said: "I had seen the photographs, I had seen the drawings and I had talked with those who are responsible for this great work, and yet I had no conception until about ten minutes ago not only of its magnitude but of its permanent beauty and permanent importance."

Two million visitors a year walk away from the monument with much the same feeling that President Roosevelt had: everyone knows what it *looks* like, but seeing it for oneself is entirely different. In real life, you are deep in the Black Hills of South Dakota—the center of the world, as far as the Lakota Indians were concerned. The smell of Ponderosa pines is in the air and the weather is not always postcard perfect. Above you are the gigantic, granite busts of four of America's most influential presidents: George Washington, Thomas Jefferson, Abraham Lincoln, and Theodore Roosevelt. They will be here for centuries and will see the destiny of the republic they helped establish and guide. Today, they're all yours.

The memorial in South Dakota was almost carved into the Needles, a unique formation of granite spires found in the Black Hills. In the 1920s, State Historian Doane Robinson was looking for a way to draw more tourism to the Black Hills. At the same time, a gigantic monument to the heroes of the Confederacy was being planned for the side of Stone Mountain in Georgia. Its sculptor was originally to be Gutzon Borglum, a renowned artist born in Idaho of Danish immigrant parents. Robinson was excited about the prospect of a memorial along the lines of Stone Mountain and thought that the Needles would make an excellent place for sculptures of American presidents.

The idea of carving up the Needles met stiff resistance from both local environmentalists and Native Americans. Borglum scouted other possible locations and decided upon Mount Rushmore in 1925.

MOUNT RUSHMORE NATIONAL MEMORIAL

March 3, 1925 • National Park Service

GREAT SMOKY MOUNTAINS NATIONAL PARK

One version of the Cherokee story of creation says that, before there was land, there was only the great stone arch of the sky above endless water. All of the animals lived in the sky, which began to get crowded. One animal, the water beetle, was brave enough to explore the water, diving deep below the surface to find mud. The water beetle brought mud to the surface, where it magically grew to be the earth. Another animal attached the mud to the sky with four rawhide ropes. When the animals wondered if the mud had dried, they sent the Great Buzzard down to the earth to make it ready. The Buzzard was tired when he arrived and his wings flapped in the mud, creating mountains and valleys. This became the Cherokee homeland.

The Cherokee were forced out of their lands in 1832 and marched to Oklahoma on the Trail of Tears. The animals remained, however, and today the Smoky Mountains are known as a place of unique biological diversity. Great Smoky Mountains National Park teems with wildlife of all kinds, from bugs to bears. At 814 square miles, the park is one of the largest areas of wild lands in the east.

At last count, there were an estimated 1,500 black bears in the park. Everyone wants to see a bear (from a distance), but the diversity of plants, invertebrates, birds, and mammals in the park has been well documented. It is one of the best places in the world to see and study salamanders, it is home to rare and endangered plants, and its streams support more than 50 species of native trout species. The national park has been working to restore several species that had previously been eliminated by overhunting and trapping, including elk, river otter, and peregrine falcons.

Its rugged scenery, diverse wildlife, 800-plus trails for hiking, 2,100 miles of streams for fishing, and 384 miles of roadway for auto touring draw nine million visitors to Great Smoky Mountains every year, making it the most heavily visited of the national parks. (The Grand Canyon is the next most popular, with 4.4 million visits in 2008.)

GREAT SMOKY MOUNTAINS NATIONAL PARK

May 22, 1926 • National Park Service

SHENANDOAH NATIONAL PARK

If you were the president of the United States in 1929, watching the nation's economy tumble into a crevasse of unprecedented depth, you would probably want to get away from the lens of public scrutiny from time to time. You would probably want to go somewhere cool and refreshing, particularly during the steamy summer months.

President Herbert Hoover certainly did: even before the stock-market crash in October of that year, Hoover was acting on the advice of his predecessor, Calvin Coolidge, and looking for a place to build a "summer White House." He found it in the Blue Ridge Mountains, in what is now Shenandoah National Park, and he built Rapidan Camp.

Sitting about 90 miles from the nation's capital and adjacent to heavily traveled and heavily urbanized interstate highway corridors, Shenandoah National Park is a refuge of wilderness and Blue Ridge peaks tucked into the starched white-collar world of northern Virginia. Shenandoah is highly accessible: its entire length can be traversed by way of Skyline Drive. This 105-mile road runs along the park's spine, reaching elevations of 3,500 feet and giving day-trippers numerous opportunities to get out at scenic overlooks and snap pictures of the nearby mountain peaks.

Non-presidential visitors to the park have a variety of options for staying overnight, including six cabins operated by the Potomac Appalachian Trail Club. Some of these cabins were built to house the workers who constructed the portion of the Appalachian Trail that runs through the area. Built in the late 1920s, they have not changed much in the past 90 years. They offer mattresses, blankets, cookware, a wood stove, a roof, and four walls: occupants must work for or carry in all other creature comforts, including potable water.

Because 40 percent of the park's nearly 200,000 acres are protected as wilderness, Shenandoah is a refuge for plants and animals that would probably have been pushed out of the area otherwise. Bats, bobcats, bears, the endangered Shenandoah salamander (found only in this park), 32 fish species, and a wide variety of wildflowers and insects can be found here.

SHENANDOAH NATIONAL PARK

May 22, 1926 • National Park Service

ARCHES NATIONAL PARK

In *Desert Solitaire*, environmentalist/anarchist Edward Abbey describes the scenery at Arches National Park as a "monstrous and inhuman spectacle of rock and cloud and sky and space." He goes on to describe his impulse to "embrace the entire scene intimately." Abbey's idea of embracing the scene goes well beyond a hike or a climb; he recommends that you "walk, better yet crawl, on hands and knees, over the sandstone and through the thornbush and cactus." While not specifically prohibited, the National Park Service would prefer that you keep activity of this sort to the marked trails.

The more than 200 natural sandstone arches here are amazing and worth the price of a good crawl. As elsewhere, however, the national parks exist both to preserve and to make these natural wonders accessible. From the Visitors Center just north of Moab in eastern Utah, the road through the park takes you to or near geologic formations that seem to defy the laws of physics.

Trails lead you further into the sandstone canyons, giving visitors an up-close look at the Devil's Garden and to the base of Delicate Arch. Biking is allowed on the trails and climbing is allowed in the park, but not on any of the named arches.

The arches were formed by the slow action of water and ice moving through sandstone, wearing away the younger parts of cliffs, leaving the denser rock above it intact to create a bridge or arch. To be considered an arch, these holes must be at least three feet wide, in any direction. At Arches National Park, some are as large as 50 feet wide.

Arches became a national monument in 1929, primarily because locals were able to convince representatives of the Rio Grande Western Railroad that the arches, if publicized and protected through the Parks Service, would bring their rail line more riders. In the long term, their hopes were thwarted by the invention of the automobile and the subsequent creation of the interstate highway system. The rail line is still there, but most visitors arrive by way of Interstate 70, which runs just north of the park.

ARCHES NATIONAL PARK

GREAT SAND DUNES NATIONAL PARK

The main dune field grows to enormous heights not only because of a complex wind regime, but also due to sand carried by Medano and Sand Creeks. These streams seasonally carve out and carry sand from the east and north side of the dune field and redeposit it where wind can transport it back to the dune field.

—National Park Service

In places vast accumulations of sand weighing millions of tons move inexorably, in regular formation, over the surface of the country, growing, retaining their shape, even breeding, in a manner which, by its grotesque imitation of life, is vaguely disturbing to the imaginative mind.

—R.A. Bagnold, F.R.S.

The sand at Great Sand Dunes National Park in south central Colorado has been pitched to the east by prevailing winds and tossed back to the west by storm winds over hundreds of millennia. Like clay thrown on a potter's wheel and guided into a graceful bowl, the winds have built the dunes up, rather than eroding them.

The dunes sit in the San Luis Valley, between the San Juan Mountains to the east and the Sangre de Cristo Mountains to the west. Ages ago, sediment from the mountains washed into a shallow lake that covered most of this valley. When the lake dried up, the sand that was left was picked up by prevailing westerly winds and pushed to the base of the Sangre de Cristo range. Storm winds howling through the mountain passes blow back to the west periodically, forcing the sand into dunes reaching as high as 750 feet.

Today, the dune field is 30 square miles and is more reminiscent of the Sahara than the Colorado wilderness. Rising above the dunes are the snow-capped Sangre de Cristos, with elevations as high as 13,000 feet.

Unlike some coastal-area dunes that are too fragile for kids to play on, the Great Sand Dunes can be climbed, rolled down, and generally frolicked upon. A plastic sled or skis work well, particularly when the dunes have seen a little rain.

The park was established in order to protect the dunes from gold mining and from being trucked away, mixed with cement and poured into the foundation of buildings as concrete. The local chapter of the Philanthropic and Educational Organization for Women (PEO) led the campaign to preserve the dunes, starting in 1930. In 1932, President Herbert Hoover signed the bill creating the Great Sand Dunes National Monument.

GREAT SAND DUNES NATIONAL PARK

EVERGLADES NATIONAL PARK

"There are no other Everglades in the world. They are, they have always been, one of the unique regions of the earth, remote, never wholly known. Nothing anywhere else is like them: their vast glittering openness, wider than the enormous visible round of the horizon, the racing free saltness and sweetness of their massive winds, under the dazzling blue heights of space."

So wrote Marjory Stoneman Douglas in her ground-breaking book *Everglades: River of Grass*, published in 1947. This book and Douglas's conservation group, Friends of the Everglades, were major forces in changing how people saw this swampy area at the southern tip of Florida.

By the time Douglas's book was published, the Everglades had long since been slated for protection, but they were still poorly understood. Everglades National Park was created largely through the efforts of one man, Ernest F. Coe, a landscape architect raised in Connecticut who moved to Florida in 1925. Coe founded the Tropical Everglades National Park Association in 1928 and successfully lobbied Stephen Mather, first director of the National Park Service, to send a team to inspect the area's merits for inclusion in the national park system. Six years later President Franklin Roosevelt approved the creation of Everglades National Forest. It was another 13 years before the park's lands could be acquired and the park was officially opened.

Water originally covered 11,000 square miles of southern Florida, including what is now Miami. Unfortunately this unique ecosystem was, and is, situated in one of the few parts of the country with both tropical weather and beachfront property. In the late 1800s and early 1900s, the swamps were drained as quickly as possible. Hundreds of miles of canals were built in the early part of the 20th century, designed to move water out.

While Everglades National Park is large—at 1.5 million acres it is the third-largest of the parks in the continental United States—it protects only a fraction of the huge ecosystem on the southern end of the peninsula. Water from Lake Okeechobee runs, very slowly, to the Gulf of Mexico by way of swampy sloughs. The flow of water in these sloughs has been measured at 100 feet per day.

The Everglades are known around the world as a wildlife refuge. Threatened and endangered species found here include the Florida panther, the West Indian manatee, four different turtle species, the American alligator, the American crocodile, and the wood stork. Additionally, there are four species of poisonous snake in the park and several species of toxic plants.

HOMESTEAD NATIONAL MONUMENT OF AMERICA

The Homestead Act of 1862 was the single most influential piece of land-use legislation in the nation's history. It affected not only how the American West was settled, but also how Americans would see themselves in the years after the Civil War. The promise of a 160-acre parcel in exchange for five years of work and building improvements on the land squared with, and perpetuated, American ideals of self-reliance and success through hard work.

The Homestead Act offered nearly everyone in the country a chance to own property. The act required that a homesteader be the head of a household or at least 21 years old. It applied to women, to immigrants, and, beginning in 1868, to African Americans.

Two hundred seventy million acres were opened up with a stroke of President Abraham Lincoln's pen. It applied to everything west of the Mississippi outside of Texas, to Alaska, and to several "eastern" states, including Florida, Mississippi, Alabama, and Ohio.

In terms of the amount of land distributed to homesteaders, Nebraska was the most successful state. Forty-five percent of its territory was parceled out to hearty sodbusters while the act was in effect.

Homestead National Monument in southeastern Nebraska was established in 1936 on the site of Daniel Freeman's homestead claim, which was filed on January 1, 1863, the day the Homestead Act became effective.

Anachronistically, it would have been possible to file a claim under the 1862 Homestead Act as recently as the mid-1980s. The act was still in effect in Alaska 10 years after its official repeal in the continental United States in 1976. The last claim under the act was filed in 1974 on 80 acres in southwestern Alaska.

To modern sensibilities, accustomed as we are to indoor plumbing, supermarkets, and industrial agriculture, the rigors of the homesteading lifestyle are virtually inconceivable. Subsisting on crops planted in the arid lands of the West, living in isolation or near a tiny agrarian community, struggling to survive seemingly endless winters and scorching summers: all of this became increasingly unpopular in the years following World War I. The Homestead Monument is a reminder of what it took to make America what it is today.

KISATCHIE NATIONAL FOREST

In those days Kisatchie was a tantalizing legend. Only a few hunters from the town of Natchitoches had hunted and camped there, and they had seen only a small portion of this wild region, hundreds of square miles in extent. The high hills may be seen across Cane River from Derry and Chopin, and they extend to within a few miles of Provencal on the north. The outcrop of Grand Gulf sandstone creates sheer stony bluffs and small waterfalls in the clear stream. Because of its heavy forests, on the oldest maps it is designated the Kisatchie Wold, a name as musical as the wind in the pines.

Immediately I began exploring this fascinating country—on horseback, in a wagon, on foot—and later in a Ford car. I saw Kistachie, Little Kisatchie, Sandy, Rocky Creek, Odom's Falls, and the tumbling waters of L'Ivorgue. The great pines came right to the Magnolia and dainty wild azalea and ferns. There the idea was born—enjoy. Since childhood my love of the kingly longleaf pines had been an obsession with me and here they grew to perfection in an idyllic setting.

[But] the lumbermen had found them and were mowing them down like fields of wheat. Because they nearly always grew in pure stands, all of merchantable size, nothing was left in the wake of the loggers. The inevitable fires followed, and the beautiful longleaf pine country was becoming a desert.

—Caroline Dormon, *The Story of Kisatchie*

In 1919, a young teacher from northern Louisiana named Caroline Dormon was sent to teach at the Kisatchie School in the state's backwoods. In her memoir *The Story of Kisatchie* she describes the area as "a tantalizing legend" that had been explored by hunters. In the 1920s, however, logging interests were taking advantage of Louisiana's thick forests and clearcutting large swaths of it.

Dormon's was one of the few voices speaking up for Kisatchie's *noncommercial* value in the 1920s, and her efforts were rewarded with the creation of this 604,000-acre national forest. While logging devastated much of the landscape in the 1920s, the Forest Service has worked to restore the area and to implement responsible logging practices.

Thanks, ultimately, to one young woman's efforts, Kisatchie has become one of the most popular sites for outdoor recreation in central Louisiana. More than 100 miles of hiking trails have been blazed through the forest and it is also known for its hunting and fishing. Off-road vehicles are allowed on designated trails in Kisatchie.

While there are no mountain peaks in Kisatchie (elevations don't get much past 300 feet here), the terrain in the Kisatchie Hills Wilderness is steep and rugged by Louisiana standards. This 8,700-acre wilderness area is the forest's real draw. Because it can only be accessed on horseback or by foot, the Wilderness offers more opportunities to see local wildlife and enjoy Kisatchie's tranquility.

BLUE RIDGE PARKWAY

For the ultimate national-parks driving experience, take the Blue Ridge Parkway from Great Smoky Mountains National Park in North Carolina to Skyline Drive in Shenandoah National Forest in Virginia. This 469-mile roadway marries these two majestic Appalachian parks and is, itself, a national park.

Like Skyline Drive, the Blue Ridge Parkway runs along mountain peaks parallel to the Appalachian Trail. From its lowest elevation of 650 feet at the James River crossing to its highest elevation of 6,047 feet in the Nantahala National Forest, the parkway is a silent tour guide, taking you to some of the best things the mountains have to offer. There are cataracts and historic homes, small mountain villages and national forests. The backdrop for everything is the verdant Appalachian Mountains, rolling away as far as the eye can see.

Work began on the parkway at Cumberland Knob in North Carolina in 1935 and was fully completed in 1987 with the opening of the Linn Cove Viaduct around Grandfather Mountain. Other than this 7.5-mile viaduct, the rest of the parkway was completed in 1967.

The National Park Service recommends planning on a four-day excursion in order to soak in all of the sights and experiences along the parkway, and with good reason: there are hundreds of things to see and do in and around this route. The trip should be savored. There are plenty of north-south interstates connecting the major population centers in the region. The parkway has a maximum speed limit of 45 miles per hour and is intended for the kind of gawking and frequent stops that are annoying to people in a hurry on other roads.

Driving from Great Smoky Mountains north, you will pass through the Cherokee Indian Reservation, the Nantahala National Forest, Mount Pisgah National Forest, Asheville (a metropolis by Blue Ridge Parkway standards, with 74,000 residents) and its endlessly diverting Folk Art Center, near Mount Mitchell State Park (the highest point east of the Mississippi), and many other smaller parks, villages, and peaks.

BOMBAY HOOK NATIONAL WILDLIFE REFUGE

If you live on or near North America's Atlantic Coast, there is a good chance that the geese you see flying overhead in the spring and fall will be making a stop at Bombay Hook National Wildlife Refuge.

This 16,000-acre sanctuary sits on the southern shore of Delaware Bay, where the fresh water of the Delaware River mingles with the Atlantic. Much of the site, about 13,000 acres, is made up of tidal salt marsh: a mix of slow-moving water, tidal pools, and mud flats. Human visitors can't see much of this area, but for migratory or nesting birds it provides excellent habitat, rich in vegetation, insects, and crustaceans. At least 250 bird species have been observed at the refuge. During the fall migration, Bombay Hook sees approximately 150,000 ducks and geese, resting on their long trip to wintering grounds.

One of the reasons Bombay Hook attracts birds is that it also attracts large numbers of horseshoe crabs. In the spring, these crabs lay their eggs on beaches and birds dig them up and feast on them. For this reason, crab monitoring has become a component of ecosystem management in this area, and horseshoe crabs can sometimes be seen crawling out of the ocean wearing small, white electronic monitoring devices.

Bombay Hook was known to Native Americans as *Canaresse*, a word meaning "at the thicket." The Dutch called it Little Tree Point, which in Dutch is *Bompies Hoeck*. The area became a national wildlife refuge in 1936, in recognition of its value as part of the migration route for eastern shorebirds. Funds to purchase the land were raised through the federal duck stamp program. Federal duck stamps are a form of hunting license for duck hunters; proceeds from the sale of these stamps are used to fund conservation.

In 1986 the Western Hemisphere Shorebird Reserve Network was created to monitor and protect important sites along migratory bird routes between Canada and Latin America. The first site identified was Delaware Bay, which was determined to be a Site of Hemispheric Importance, sheltering 500,000 birds annually.

BOMBAY HOOK NATIONAL WILDLIFE REFUGE

June 22, 1937 • U.S. Fish and Wildlife Service

SARATOGA NATIONAL HISTORICAL PARK

The story of the American victory over the British in the farm fields and wooded hills near Saratoga, New York, just north of the Hudson River, is a classic piece of military history. Topography, military engineering, lines of reinforcement, poor communication, luck, and, above all, egos converged here in September and October 1777, and the Americans' victory has often been called the turning point in the Revolutionary War.

The battlefield preserved by Saratoga National Historical Park covers about 3,000 acres and visitors can drive a nine-mile self-guided tour through its key locations.

The two clashes that are collectively referred to as "the Battles of Saratoga" took place on September 19 and October 7, 1777. The British objective was control of the Hudson River, and the British commander, General John Burgoyne, believed that this could be accomplished by marching south from Lake Champlain along the Hudson River road and meeting up with two other British armies that he believed were en route to Albany. Unfortunately for Burgoyne, the overall strategy was thwarted by miscommunication and misfortune: the other two armies never arrived and his force of 7,000 was left alone to tackle the Americans defending the Hudson.

Nevertheless, Burgoyne took the critical American outpost at Fort Ticonderoga in July 1777, and he might have been successful in marching to Albany had it not been for a Polish military engineer, Colonel Thaddeus Kosciuszko, who fortified a position on the Hudson that forced the British to turn away from the river, to the west. This brought the British into contact with the Americans at Freeman's Farm on September 19. The Continental Army, commanded by General Horatio Gates, stopped the British advance but did not win the field. The British established fortifications and waited for reinforcements that were not coming.

On October 7, with his army reduced in number by losses in the previous battle and by subsequent desertions, Burgoyne decided to try an assault on the American position. Estimates are that his force numbered 6,800 and that the American force had grown from 8,500 in September to 13,000 in October. Burgoyne's attack was repulsed and the British retreated behind their fortifications. The American counterpunch failed to take the southernmost fortification, Balcarres Redoubt, but the assault on the other, Breymann Redoubt, was successful.

One of the most interesting aspects of the American advance on the 7th is the notoriety it won for the already celebrated, and almost certainly egomaniacal, General Benedict Arnold. Arnold made a reckless charge between the two British artillery fortifications, during which he was wounded in the leg. Today, visitors to the battlefield often scratch their heads over the monument there that commemorates Arnold's leg wound.

SHAWNEE NATIONAL FOREST

The Shawnee is one of a score of Eastern national forests established during the Great Depression. The Shawnee was established, in part, to help improve the lot of [impoverished farm] families. . . . These Depression Era–New Deal forests were established to achieve broad social goals—to relieve human suffering and help the nation recover from painful economic distress. The Shawnee is another success story; worn-out farmland has been returned to forest and made productive once again.

—William D. Shands, "National Forests and the Human Legacy: Some History"

In southern Illinois, the Ozark and Shawnee mountains interrupt the region's cornfields and ruler-straight roads. Erosion and weathering have created interesting rock formations here and preservation efforts have allowed forests to reclaim the land. As a result, the Shawnee National Forest has become one of the foremost sites for outdoor recreation in the state.

Natural attractions include the Little Grand Canyon, rock outcroppings in the Garden of the Gods and the Devil's Backbone, and numerous waterfalls. Hiking is probably the most popular activity, but the forest is also an excellent place for horseback riding.

The 160-mile River-to-River Trail connects the Mississippi and Ohio rivers; much of this hiking trail is also open to equestrian use. The trail connects many of the forest's prominent features and is part of the American Discovery Trail, which extends from California to Delaware.

Hiking, climbing, fishing, hunting, or camping in the park may bring you face-to-face with the local wildlife. This can get dangerous, since copperheads, rattlesnakes, and water moccasins can all be found in this area. Other, fuzzier residents include beaver, fox, and muskrats.

Efforts to preserve the forest began in the early 1930s after farming had depleted the soils and reckless timber-harvesting practices had made soil erosion a serious concern. Shawnee National Forest was dedicated by Franklin Roosevelt in 1939.

SHAWNEE NATIONAL FOREST

September 6, 1939 • U.S. Forestry Service

CUMBERLAND GAP NATIONAL HISTORICAL PARK

Walking into the Cumberland Gap today, cell phone in hand and taking occasional sips from a bottle of water, visitors must strain their imaginations to understand the importance of this Appalachian Mountains pass to early American history. During the Civil War, Ulysses Grant described it as "the American Gibraltar."

While the Gap's strategic importance during the War Between the States was limited to a few minor skirmishes, Grant's expression was apt. It is the best crossing of the Appalachians for hundreds of miles to its north and south. The Wilderness Road blazed by Daniel Boone and, before it, the Warriors' Path of the Native Americans, ran through the Gap, connecting what are now Virginia and North Carolina to Kentucky and Tennessee. In the 18th century, this meant a connection between settled areas and a huge, unknown frontier.

Daniel Boone and a small group of men, hired by a land company to establish a route through the Cumberland Gap, began cutting the Wilderness Road through the virgin mountain forests in March 1775. In the book *The Adventures of Colonel Daniel Boone*, published in 1784, he describes the frontier and the new road's effect on it:

> Thus we behold Kentucky, lately an howling wilderness, the habitation of savages and wild beasts, become a fruitful field; this region, so favourably distinguished by nature, now become the habitation of civilization, at a period unparalleled in history, in the midst of a raging war, and under all the disadvantages of emigration to a country so remote from the inhabited parts of the continent.

After the Revolutionary War, settlers trickled through the Cumberland Gap and along the primitive Wilderness Road. The Native American inhabitants of the area were the Shawnee to the north and the Cherokee to the south. Neither were occupying southeastern Kentucky at the time, but both had long used the area as a hunting ground and periodically warred for control of the area. The arrival of white settlers was unwelcome to these early inhabitants and led to raids against them and wars against the Indians.

Like water finding a hole in a dam, 300,000 settlers poured through the Gap in the latter part of the 1700s. Today, Cumberland Gap National Historical Park sits on 20,000 acres at the intersection of Kentucky, Tennessee, and Virginia. In addition to the Gap itself, there are hiking trails through the mountains and tours of fascinating caves.

CUMBERLAND GAP NATIONAL HISTORICAL PARK

HARPERS FERRY NATIONAL HISTORICAL PARK

Viewed from the surrounding hills, the little community on the point of land at the confluence of the Shenandoah and Potomac rivers looks peaceful and content. Sunlight sparkles on the two rivers, oaks and poplars shade the river banks, and red brick buildings line narrow streets. But Harpers Ferry, located as it is at the borders of West Virginia, Virginia, and Maryland, was a lightning rod for political and military activity in the second half of the 19th century.

Harpers Ferry is best known to history as the site of John Brown's raid of the federal arsenal there, and his attempt to lead an armed uprising of black slaves. Brown's raiding party of 21 men (5 black and 16 white) crossed the Potomac on October 16, 1859. Their plan was to arm themselves using the guns at the arsenal and to head south into the Appalachian Mountains, starting a guerilla offensive to create an army of freed slaves in Virginia.

The raiding party was able to cut the town's telegraph wires, take several hostages, and capture the arsenal. Within two days federal troops (led, in one of history's quirks, by Colonel Robert E. Lee) had Brown surrounded and, wounded in the leg, he surrendered. Brown was tried for treason, found guilty, and hanged in Virginia that December.

Less than two years later, the Civil War came to Harpers Ferry. Union troops burned the federal arsenal to keep it out of Confederate hands. Confederates destroyed factory buildings and a railroad bridge to keep them out of Union hands. The little village flipped between Union and Confederate control eight times during the war.

In 1906, John Brown's legacy in Harpers Ferry was revived, in the form of the first meeting of the Niagara Movement in the United States. The Niagara Movement was the forerunner of the National Association for the Advancement of Colored People. The group chose Harper's Ferry as a meeting place in part because of the symbolic significance of Brown's actions.

THEODORE ROOSEVELT NATIONAL PARK

The young Theodore Roosevelt described the terrain of his ranch in North Dakota in his 1885 book *Hunting Trips of a Ranchman:*

From the edges of the valley the land rises abruptly in steep high buttes whose crests are sharp and jagged. This broken country extends back from the river for many miles, and has been called always, by Indians, French voyageurs, and American trappers alike, the "Bad Lands," partly from its dreary and forbidding aspect and partly from the difficulty experienced in travelling through it.

Roosevelt stepped into this rugged landscape at the age of 25, primarily interested in hunting bison. After meeting local ranchers and becoming convinced that cattle ranching in this desolate land was a good investment, he bought the Maltese Cross Ranch. This and his other ranch, Elkhorn, were not great moneymakers, but the toughness of the land was a good fit for the young man's dynamism.

His time as a rancher and his travels between New York and North Dakota also gave him a much better sense than most other easterners had of what was happening to the Midwest and West in the 1880s. Human settlement was increasingly moving into previously wild land with devastating consequences for the land's beauty. As president, Roosevelt created the U.S. Forest Service, approved the 1906 American Antiquities Act (which allowed the creation of national monuments), and protected an estimated 230 million acres of land.

Theodore Roosevelt National Park is as much about preserving the land and wildlife there as it is remembering the man and a chapter in his life that shaped his attitude toward conservation. This is not to give the park's land and wildlife short shrift. The wildlife, particularly, draws visitors to this area: bison herds, prairie dogs, wild mustangs, and golden eagles can all be found here. The park is split into three units: the Southern Unit, the Northern Unit, and Elk Ranch. The Northern and Elk Ranch units are less accessible and, therefore, less heavily traveled.

THEODORE ROOSEVELT NATIONAL PARK

February 25, 1946 • National Park Service

FORT MOULTRIE (FORT SUMTER NATIONAL MONUMENT)

The wooden logs of the fort on Sullivan's Island were still being put in place when it was attacked by British ships in June 1776. Amazingly the fort, which had not yet been named, was able to withstand the bombardment. Had the British succeeded in smashing its defenses, they could have sailed into Charleston Harbor and taken South Carolina's capitol, Charles Town (today known as Charleston). After the Battle of Sullivan's Island, the fort was named in honor of its commander, Colonel William Moultrie.

After the Revolutionary War, the original Fort Moultrie declined, was rebuilt, was swept away by a hurricane, and was rebuilt again. On the eve of the Civil War, it was the headquarters for the U.S. Army garrison in Charleston. Because Fort Moultrie was poorly equipped to deal with an attack from land, its strategic importance had largely been eclipsed by the newer Fort Sumter, being built on an island in the middle of the harbor's entrance.

South Carolina was the first state to secede from the Union after Abraham Lincoln won the presidency in November 1860. The South Carolina legislature voted for secession on December 20, 1860. Six days later the federal soldiers at Fort Moultrie, expecting the need to defend themselves from local militias, slipped out to Fort Sumter.

Fort Moultrie then became part of the siege of Fort Sumter, which lasted until April 1861. In the early morning hours of April 13, Confederate cannon began shelling Fort Sumter from several nearby forts, including Moultrie. On April 14, the troops in Fort Sumter surrendered with no loss of life on either side.

In the years following the Civil War, the defenses at Fort Moultrie were improved to keep pace with improvements to military technology. Ultimately, a larger complex of concrete and steel fortifications known as Fort Moultrie Military Reservation was established on Sullivan's Island.

Today, Fort Moultrie is part of Fort Sumter National Monument. The Fort Moultrie portion of the park gives visitors a sense of the progression of military technology there.

Fort Moultrie (Fort Sumter National Monument)

April 28, 1948 • National Park Service

EFFIGY MOUNDS NATIONAL MONUMENT

Preserved at Effigy Mounds National Monument on bluffs above the Mississippi River are 206 prehistoric mounds, more than 30 of which are built in the shape of animals. The exact purpose of the mounds is unknown, but similar mounds are found throughout southern Wisconsin, southeastern Minnesota, and northeastern Iowa. These mysterious artifacts of a vanished culture are reminders that North America is a land with a history that begins well before 1492—and even before the collective memory of the Native American peoples who were here then.

Mound development is believed to have progressed through several phases. The oldest at Effigy Mounds are conical, dating to roughly 2,500 years ago. They are relatively large, between 10 and 20 feet in diameter and 2 to 8 feet high. Later came so-called linear mounds, built to be 6 to 8 feet across and 2 to 4 feet high. In some cases, these linear mounds connect conical mounds to form long "compound" mounds.

What really attracts attention are the large effigy mounds. At Effigy Mounds, these primarily take bear or bird shapes. While the mounds are not very high, they are very large. One of the bird mounds has a wingspan of 212 feet. The Great Bear Mound is less than 4 feet high, but is 137 feet long and 70 feet wide.

The mounds are generally believed to be burial-related, but archaeologists studying similar mounds in the region periodically excavate effigy mounds in which no trace of burial remains can be found. According to Native American tradition, the mounds were sacred ceremonial sites, but the exact nature of the ceremonies is still unclear. One aspect of the mounds that often captures the imagination of modern visitors is that they really don't look like much from the ground: they are best viewed from above.

The National Park Service encourages visitors to be mindful that they are in a special place, a sacred burial site. There are no 50-foot observation towers or automobile tours here—just quiet trails under basswood and sugar maples.

FREDERICK DOUGLASS NATIONAL HISTORIC SITE

I have been frequently asked how I felt when I found myself in a free State. I have never been able to answer the question with any satisfaction to myself. It was a moment of the highest excitement I ever experienced. I suppose I felt as one may imagine the unarmed mariner to feel when he is rescued by a friendly man-of-war from the pursuit of a pirate.

—Frederick Douglass, *Narrative of the Life of Frederick Douglass, an American Slave*

In 1838, after his two previous attempts at escape had failed, Frederick Douglass made a third, very risky attempt at escaping slavery. With borrowed papers in his pocket identifying him as a free black in the U.S. Navy, and disguised as a sailor, he hopped on a train. The next day he was free, living in New York City. Through his autobiographical writings and speaking tours both in the United States and Europe, Douglass became one of the most influential figures of the 19th century.

Born a slave in rural Maryland around 1818, Douglass was taught to read and write by Sophia Auld, his master's wife, when he was about 12 years old. He was later moved to Baltimore and sent to work in the shipyards there. In Baltimore, he met free black Anna Murray, and the two were married after his escape from Maryland.

Frederick and Anna settled in New England where, in 1841, he became a traveling speaker for the Massachusetts Anti-Slavery Society. His description of the degrading effects of slavery—on both slave and slave owner—gave abolitionists in the northeast new ammunition with which to attack the "peculiar institution."

Douglass published his first autobiography, *Narrative of the Life of Frederick Douglass, an American Slave,* in 1845. It was an immediate sensation that led to international acclaim and a speaking tour of England and Ireland. He later published his own abolitionist newspaper, *The North Star,* and became a leader in the abolitionist movement. Significantly, his views on freedom extended beyond freedom for slaves: he was the only African American at the 1848 Women's Rights Convention in Seneca Falls, and spoke in favor of women's suffrage.

The house in Anacostia in Washington, D.C., that is now the site of the national historic monument was Douglass's home after the Civil War, from 1878 until his death in 1895.

OZARK NATIONAL SCENIC RIVERWAYS

Ozark National Scenic Riverways, formed by the Current and Jack Fork rivers, was the first national park founded to protect a wild river system. The rivers are fed by more than 300 springs, including the largest concentration of first-magnitude springs in the world. A first-magnitude spring has a flow of at least 65 million gallons of water per day. The aptly named Big Spring has a daily water flow of 286 million gallons! The springs, especially Blue Spring, are a particularly beautiful shade of blue.

The park is home to hundreds of caves. Some, like the magnificent Jam Up Cave, can be reached only by boat. At the other end of the spectrum, rangers lead tours of Round Spring Cavern twice daily during the summer months.

The wildlife congregating near these springs and caves is incredibly varied. Several rare species of fish, found only in the Ozarks, swim in the rivers. Rare plants that survived the Ice Age grow in the cool crags of the bluffs above the rivers. On the banks, white-tailed deer and wild turkeys mingle with collared lizards, tarantulas, and scorpions.

In addition to its natural wonders, the park includes several man-made sites of interest. The ruins of Welch Hospital stand at the entrance to Welch Cave and Spring. The hospital was built in 1913 by a doctor who believed that the spring water and cool cave air would benefit people suffering from lung diseases. The hospital limped along unsuccessfully until the doctor's death in 1945. The concept was doomed by the refusal of any other doctors to endorse dank cave air as a cure-all for tuberculosis, and by the onerous journey that was necessary for consumptive patients to reach the remote site.

In the town of Alley, visitors can tour a mill constructed in 1894, visit a one-room schoolhouse, or shop at the old-fashioned general store.

The park is a popular recreation destination. There are several campgrounds, ranging from primitive sites to cabins constructed in the 1930s by the Civilian Conservation Corps, to larger campgrounds with modern amenities and ranger programs. Hunting and fishing are allowed in portions of the park. The biggest recreational draw is a float trip on the spring-fed rivers. Canoe rentals are widely available, with many of the park's most interesting and unusual sites best viewed from the river. But if you're coming to float, leave your keg and wine bottles at home. In response to the community's complaints about rowdy behavior on the rivers, the park's superintendent has imposed new rules and regulations to ensure a more serene and family-friendly atmosphere.

ELLIS ISLAND NATIONAL MONUMENT (STATUE OF LIBERTY)

On a cold New Year's Day, in 1892, a young girl named Annie Moore from County Cork, Ireland, was welcomed into Ellis Island Immigration Station. She was the first of more than 12 million immigrants to enter the United States through that gateway until its closure in 1952. Ellis Island replaced the immigration station at Castle Garden, which had been in operation since 1855.

Tumultuous events in Europe, including the potato famine in Ireland and political unrest in Germany, were the "stick" driving immigrants out of the Old World. Opportunities in America, such as the Homestead Act of 1862, were the "carrot," attracting Europeans to New York in ever-increasing numbers. By the end of the 1800s, the federal government had taken over control of immigration, which previously had been a state function. The large numbers of people entering through New York prompted the construction of the buildings on Ellis Island, which had been used sporadically by the military since the War of 1812.

In June 1897 a fire destroyed the main registration building on Ellis Island. After a three-year closure, the station was reopened with the buildings that stand there today.

Immigration stations like Ellis Island and Castle Garden were designed as checks on the spread of disease and the entrance of undesirable immigrants into the country; the poorest arrivals, not members of the upper classes, were screened at these stations. Anyone wealthy enough to afford a first- or second-class ticket on a transatlantic ship was considered sufficiently healthy and respectable to enter the country, and their papers were approved on board the ship.

Anyone suspected of having a disease like tuberculosis or of being mentally incompetent and likely to become a ward of the state would be detained for further examination. Suspected criminals and, oddly, polygamists could also be denied entrance. A healthy person with papers in order could pass through Ellis Island in three or four hours. After that, the opportunities of a new land lay open.

ELLIS ISLAND NATIONAL MONUMENT (STATUE OF LIBERTY)

May 11, 1965 • National Park Service

GEORGE ROGERS CLARK NATIONAL HISTORICAL PARK

When George Rogers Clark and his band of 130 men arrived under cover of darkness in Vincennes, on the Wabash River in present-day Indiana, they must have been on the verge of collapse. Bent on surprising the small British force at Fort Sackville, Clark had organized a daring 18-day march across 180 miles of untamed frontier in the middle of February.

The year was 1779 and the British had control of virtually all of the land in the Ohio River Valley west of the Appalachians. With their Indian allies, the British were organizing raids on any American settlements found in Kentucky or the Old Northwest—the area ringing the Great Lakes west of New York and Pennsylvania.

Clark, a lieutenant colonel in the Virginia militia at the age of 25, was charged with the defense of these settlements and was determined to end the raids by taking up the offensive.

Because it was winter, the British commander at Fort Sackville, Lieutenant Governor Henry Hamilton, had allowed some of the fort's guards to return to their homes until spring. Clark's maneuver was a complete surprise, and he was able to surround the fort. Upon capturing an Indian raid party that was returning to the fort, Clark had five members of the party killed in full view of the British in order to demonstrate his capacity for cruelty to his enemies. Soon afterward, the British surrendered.

Control of Fort Sackville gave Clark the ability to parry other British offensives for the remainder of the Revolutionary War and established an American military presence in this region until 1814, when the British formally relinquished their claim to the Northwest Territory.

George Rogers Clark National Historical Park is a monument to a patriot's fighting spirit. Clark, whose younger brother William explored the far west with Meriwether Lewis, is memorialized in a bronze statue. The statue was sculpted by an artist named Hermon Atkins MacNeil, whose most famous work is probably the Standing Liberty quarter, minted from 1916 to 1930.

...EVOLUTION ★ THE CONQUEST OF THE WE...

ERECTED BY
THE UNITED STATES
ON LAND PROVIDED BY
THE STATE OF INDIANA
THE COUNTY OF KNOX
THE CITY OF VINCENNES
MCMXXXI

GEORGE ROGERS CLARK NATIONAL HISTORICAL PARK

July 23, 1966 • National Park Service

PICTURED ROCKS NATIONAL LAKESHORE

> *. . . For Pau-Puk-Keewis,*
> *Once again in human figure,*
> *Full in sight ran on before him,*
> *Sped away in gust and whirlwind,*
> *On the shores of Gitche Gumee,*
> *Westward by the Big-Sea-Water,*
> *Came unto the rocky headlands,*
> *To the Pictured Rocks of sandstone,*
> *Looking over lake and landscape.*
>
> **—Henry Wadsworth Longfellow,**
> **"The Song of Hiawatha"**

Forty-two miles of Lake Superior shoreline are preserved in Pictured Rocks National Lakeshore. The star attractions at this park are the 200-foot sandstone cliffs rising above the lake. Their sedimentary bands are eye-catching, with alternating lines of dark orange, light brown, and shades in between. Where the cliffs are interrupted by waterfalls tumbling into the lake, the scenery becomes some of the best that Lake Superior can offer.

Pictured Rocks was the first designated national lakeshore. The National Park Service started looking for possible sites on the Great Lakes in the late 1950s. The park's report described the "unique and spectacular scenery unmatched elsewhere on the Great Lakes" at Pictured Rocks. After several years of planning, President Lyndon Johnson approved the park's creation in 1966.

In addition to lakeshore, this park preserves nearly 34,000 acres of Michigan's Upper Peninsula. Short trails lead to sites such as Grand Sable Dunes, covering five square miles on the park's northeastern end, and to Miner's Castle, the park's most famous rock formation.

Commercial boat tours troll along the cliffs, but experienced kayakers can get a much more intimate look at the cliffs from the surface of the lake. There are four put-ins for kayaks within the park. Because of the potential for rough waters, canoes and small boats are impractical on Lake Superior (remember that this is the lake that swallowed the *Edmund Fitzgerald*). But a small boat is the perfect way to get to know the three lakes in the park: Beaver Lake, Little Beaver Lake, and Grand Sable Lake.

Longer trails connect most of the sites in this sprawling park, giving backpackers ample opportunity to get to know the lakeshore's forests, waterfalls, wetlands, and wildlife. Animals that have been spotted here include moose, lynx, red fox, fisher, and badger.

PICTURED ROCKS NATIONAL LAKESHORE

October 15, 1966 • National Park Service

APOSTLE ISLANDS NATIONAL LAKESHORE

It is of trees and water and beauty that people think when they remember the Apostle Islands. And indeed, these are the dominant shaping forces in the lakeshore. But the lakeshore is more than the trees and the lake. Millions of years of geologic history are written in the islands. The advance and retreat of glaciers during the Pleistocene Era carved the islands and the peninsula out of Precambrian sandstone, exposing beautiful white sand beaches, dramatic cliffs, sculpted shorelines, and water-worn caves.

—**Harold C. Jordahl Jr.,** *A Unique Collection of Islands*

If a sea kayak wasn't on your shopping list prior to visiting the Apostle Islands, you'll probably find yourself trying to find space for one after you leave. The best way to get to know Apostle Islands National Lakeshore is by boat.

There are more than 50 miles of trails in the park, but most of them are on the islands; there is one 4.5-mile trail on the mainland. In the summer, sea kayaking gives experienced paddlers the ideal way to get to know the park's many islands and the mainland's intriguing sea caves.

One extremely alluring aspect of Apostle Islands is the transformation of its sandstone caves from sea caves to ice caves in the depth of winter. When Lake Superior freezes the caves can be explored on foot; the Visitor's Center provides periodic updates on how thick the ice is and whether or not this activity is advisable. For those willing to endure a mile-long hike across a blinding-white, frozen lake, the payoff is a chance to walk around in this otherworldly environment of ice and rock.

Another of Apostle Islands' unique features is Stockton Island, home to one of the largest concentrations of black bears in North America: around two dozen are likely to be present at any time. Stockton Island is one of the most popular of the islands in the park. The 14 miles of maintained trails lead from the Visitor's Center, at Presque Isle, over a natural sand bridge called a *tombolo*, to the main island. From there, a trail leads to the site of the brownstone quarry that was heavily mined here in the late 1800s.

Scuba diving is popular in this park, providing another way to get into the islands' sea caves and the only way to see underwater rock formations like submerged sandstone ledges. It is also the only way to explore the shipwrecks sitting on the bottom of the lake near the islands.

Apostle Islands National Lakeshore • 415 Washington Avenue, Bayfield, Wisconsin, 54814

APOSTLE ISLANDS NATIONAL LAKESHORE

September 26, 1970 • National Park Service

VOYAGEURS NATIONAL PARK

The "Voyageur's Highway" that threaded [the] vast northern wilderness included some 120 exhausting portages, 200 treacherous rapids, and 50 lakes large enough that stormy weather could imperil even the big "Montreal" canoes. At Rainy Lake, on the present boundary between Minnesota and Ontario, voyageurs on the eastward journey from the interior met crews on the westward journey from Montreal, exchanged cargoes, and turned around. . . . The French-Canadian voyageurs paddled up to 16 hours a day, made encampments, traded with Indians, and sometimes met death and a lonely burial.

—**Ted Catton, *Special History: The Environment and the Fur Trade Experience in Voyageurs National Park, 1730–1870***

When Jacques de Noyon reached the Rainy Lakes region west of Lake Superior in 1688, he saw the scenery and wildlife there very much as they are today. Then, as now, moose could be seen browsing on shrubs in small groups in the marshy lowlands, packs of timber wolves could be spotted periodically and heard much more frequently, and the tracks of beaver, fox, muskrat, and other fur-bearers were plentiful.

Noyon was a *coureur-des-bois* (literally "runner of the words"), a French-Canadian fur trader who was pushing west to trade with the Ojibwe Indians. Like the Indians he made his way in a birch-bark canoe, using an extensive system of waterways and portages. The coureurs-des-bois were unlicensed traders who were essentially trying to short-circuit the existing trade system between Native Americans and fur buyers in Montreal, cutting out the middlemen. In French-Canadian lore, they are generally described as young cavaliers more interested in adventure than profit. Later, Montreal issued licenses to these traders and trappers, who became known as the voyageurs.

The area known today as Voyageurs National Park on the Minnesota-Canada border was preserved, largely, thanks to the efforts of Ernest Oberholtzer, one of the founding members of the Wilderness Society. Oberholtzer came to Rainy Lake in the early 1900s and fell in love with canoeing on the lakes. He settled there in 1915. Ten years later, a local paper and lumber producer proposed a system of federally funded dams on the area's waterways for flood control. Testifying in front of Congress, Oberholtzer managed to persuade the politicians that the region was worth preserving.

Like Noyon and Oberholtzer, visitors to Voyageurs National Park have the most fun when they get out on the water. The park rents canoes and rowboats. The waterways are endless and 200 boat-in campsites are available.

VOYAGEURS NATIONAL PARK

January 8, 1971 • National Park Service

CUMBERLAND ISLAND NATIONAL SEASHORE

Cumberland Island is probably one of the most purely restful national parks in the continental United States. Recreation here is of the hiking, swimming, and beachcombing variety, rather than the more strenuous pursuits of other parks. There are no mountains to climb, no spelunking opportunities, no deserts to traverse.

The white-sand beaches are largely undeveloped and wide open for at-your-own-risk swimming. Beachcombers regularly find sharks' teeth and are free to collect up to two gallons of (unoccupied) shells, as well as dead starfish and other souvenirs.

There are no distracted tourists driving oversized vehicles on the island, because no vehicles of any kind are allowed on the ferry and most visitors get to the island by way of the ferry. After you reach Cumberland Island, it's you, the waves, the wildlife, and a 17-mile-long island waiting to be explored.

The one catch is that, unlike many national parks, you need a reservation to get in. This is not to say it's "exclusive," but you do need to plan ahead. The Park Service limits the number of visitors to 300 at a time and limits each overnight camper to a maximum of seven nights. Part of the park's purpose is to maintain the island in an undisturbed state. At 36,000 acres, the National Seashore portion of the island is not endless: there are a limited number of campsites. Visitors take a ferry to the island and no one is allowed on the ferry without a reservation.

The trails are fairly extensive for a relatively small island. There are 50 miles of hiking trails, including the north-south Grand Avenue, leading through a living tunnel of healthy oak boughs. At the northern end of the island is the area known as The Settlement, where black workers lived beginning in the 1890s. One of the remaining structures is the tiny First African Baptist Church, where John F. Kennedy Jr. married Carolyn Bessette in 1996.

While the Kennedy family never owned land on Cumberland Island, the Carnegies did. The ruins of the mansion called Dungeness, built by Thomas Carnegie, brother of Andrew, are on the island's southern end, just above the marshes and ponds at the tip of the island. Carnegie's Dungeness was built on the site of an earlier mansion of the same name, which deteriorated in the years after the Civil War.

BLOCK ISLAND NATIONAL WILDLIFE REFUGE

It lies so far out in the sea that in summer its surface is cooled by the most refreshing breezes and in winter its hills are swept by fearful gales and its shores are wreathed with the white foam of assaulting billows. . . . No person ever saw the surface of the ocean more uneven than is the land of Block Island, excepting those who witnessed the flood in the days of Noah. It is necessary to resort to the imagination to give an adequate view of this extraordinary unevenness which puts this Island among the natural curiosities to the observer.

—Samuel Truesdale Livermore,
***A History of Block Island* (1877)**

Block Island National Wildlife Refuge is a resting place for migratory songbirds using the Atlantic flyway. In spring and fall, the trill of the song sparrow and the calls of 70 other songbird species can be heard here. In summer, tiger swallowtail and other butterflies appear. In late September the annual monarch butterfly migration brings those winged visitors to the island. The annual bird and butterfly migrations draw birders and other wildlife fanatics to this refuge like paparazzi.

Block Island sits in the Atlantic Ocean about 13 miles south of Rhode Island and 14 miles east of Long Island. The island has a permanent population of about 1,000 (human) residents, but its extensive beaches and historic buildings draw large crowds in the summer.

The national wildlife refuge was created in 1973 using 28 acres from the U.S. Coast Guard. Donations and purchases have increased it to its current size of 129 acres. The easiest way to reach the island is by catching the ferry from Narrangansett, Rhode Island. There are no trails in the refuge—visitors are generally free to prowl around at their leisure.

Few visitors will probably get a chance to see the lovely American burying beetle, but Block Island is believed to support the only population of this insect east of the Mississippi River. The beetle is easily identified by the striking, bright-orange spots on its back.

In addition to being on the southward flight path for birds from Nova Scotia, Block Island's importance to migrating songbirds is due in part because it provides a refuge for small songbirds that get pushed off their southern route by strong winds. Landing at this island gives them a chance to eat and rest before resuming their migration.

Block Island National Wildlife Refuge is one of the five sites in the Rhode Island National Wildlife Refuge Complex. The other four refuges are on the mainland, in coastal areas.

LOWELL NATIONAL HISTORICAL PARK

Sent to work in Lowell, Massachusetts, when she was 11 years old, author and poet Lucy Larcom would later describe life in the mill in her memoir, *A New England Girlhood*. The water-powered mills in Lowell were cutting-edge for their time and are considered the beginning of Industrial Revolution technology in America, but to a young girl, they didn't look like much. She says:

> I never cared much for machinery. The buzzing and hissing and whizzing of pulleys and rollers and spindles and flyers around me often grew tiresome. I could not see into their complications, or feel interested in them. But in a room below us we were sometimes allowed to peer in through a sort of blind door at the great water-wheel that carried the works of the whole mill. It was so huge that we could only watch a few of its spokes at a time, and part of its dripping rim, moving with a slow, measured strength through the darkness that shut it in.

Water, drawn away from nearby Pawtucket Falls through a system of canals, made the mills in Lowell possible: water wheels were the power system. The other half of the equation was the machines, the looms, that received that power and used it to convert cotton into textiles.

The water-powered textile mill was not invented in Massachusetts, but it was reinvented or, as we might say today, reverse engineered in Waltham, Massachusetts, by the team of Francis Cabot Lowell and Paul Moody. Lowell had toured the mills of Britain in 1810, and he worked with Moody, a mechanic, to recreate what he had seen. They were brilliantly successful. The new machines were part of the Boston Manufacturing Company's mill in Waltham, built in 1814. Lowell and his partners made a lot of money and began making plans to recreate their success on a larger scale. Unfortunately, Lowell himself died three years later.

In the 1820s, the heads of the Boston Manufacturing Company bought up farmland near what was then East Chelmsford, near Pawtucket Falls. Planning for a robust operation, they built large dormitories to house workers (primarily young women, called "Mill Girls") and attempted to build a new kind of factory town that would be an improvement over similar complexes in Britain, which had been hotbeds of unrest. Lowell's former partners renamed East Chelmsford in his honor.

Between 1820 and 1850, dozens of other mills sprouted up in Lowell, drawing thousands of new workers to the area and forever transforming how things were made in America. Lowell National Historical Park was established in the 1970s both to preserve this history and to give this aging mill town a shot in the arm.

AMERICAN MEMORIAL PARK

With Saipan secured on July, 1944, U.S. Forces were able to cut off vital Japanese supply and communication lines, and American B-29 bombers moved within range of the Japanese homeland. For most of the soldiers, seamen, and airmen it was yet another invasion. For many it would be their last. For the world it was the beginning of the end of the Pacific War.

—National Park Service

The commander of the American Marine Force in the Pacific referred to Operation Forager, which included the battles of Saipan and Tinian, as "the decisive battle of the Pacific Offensive." At Saipan, approximately 70,000 Americans fought 30,000 Japanese using weapons ranging from fast modern battleships to flamethrowers to bayonets. When it was over three weeks later, 13,000 Americans had been killed and wounded and nearly the entire Japanese garrison was dead, either through wounds sustained in battle or by suicide. Thousands of Japanese civilians either chose or were forced by Japanese officers to jump to their deaths off of Banzai Cliff and Suicide Cliff.

American Memorial Park includes somber memorials to the American servicemen and Marianas natives who died in this decisive battle. These memorials include a court of honor listing the names of the more than 5,000 service personnel who died during the Marianas Campaign; a flag circle comprised of a 48-star American flag and the flags of each branch of the American armed services; and a carillon bell tower that chimes every half hour.

The park prides itself as a "living memorial." Visitors are encouraged to partake of activities that young men and women of the 1940s would have enjoyed, such as baseball games on the park's specially built field, a tennis match on one of the four lighted courts, sunbathing on the white-sand beaches, a concert at the park's large amphitheater, or a picnic with admirable views. The well-groomed roads and trails are popular with joggers and cyclists. In addition to these time-honored activities, the park's Micro Beach is considered one of the world's best windsurfing sites.

The Visitor Center opened in 2005 and includes exhibits about pre-war life on Saipan, the war, the battle, and the aftermath. It highlights the experiences and contributions of the natives of the Marianas, the Chomorros and Carolinians.

WAR IN THE PACIFIC NATIONAL HISTORICAL PARK

Guam, a 200-square-mile island in the western Pacific, was the site of some of the fiercest fighting in World War II. Three days after the attack on Pearl Harbor, Japanese special forces landed on Guam and overwhelmed the lightly armed U.S. Marines, Guardsmen, and Navy personnel holding the island. Three years later, the Americans returned in force. On July 21, 1944, the first Marines landed. By the time the battle ended on August 4, more than 7,000 Americans had been killed or wounded. More than 18,000 Japanese soldiers kept their vow to die fighting. Their commander committed seppuku on August 11, 1944. Approximately 1,000 Japanese soldiers hid in the jungle rather than surrendering or committing suicide. One such soldier, Shoichi Yokoi, remained hidden in the jungle until he was discovered by hunters in 1972.

The American victory at Guam was one of the turning points in the War in the Pacific. The strategic value of Guam and the other Mariana islands was so great that when he received word of the American victory, Japanese admiral Miwa confided to Emperor Hirohito that "hell is upon us."

War in the Pacific National Historic Park is a unique memorial to the battle of Guam and the other battles that raged in the Pacific Theater. The park includes the expected tributes to America and its allies: the Memorial Wall at the Asia Bay Overlook lists the names of the 16,142 American and Chamorro (the natives of Guam) dead and wounded, while the Liberator's Memorial honors those who participated in the 1944 retaking of Guam. However, the park also explicitly honors the bravery and sacrifices of all who participated in Pacific battles, including the Japanese.

The park includes more than 100 historical sites from the World War II, including bunkers, pill boxes, and defensive guns. In addition, the park is a place of great natural beauty. Scuba diving and snorkeling are permitted in the warm Pacific waters, where visitors may encounter the endangered hawksbill sea turtle, the threatened green sea turtle, or 3,500 other marine species.

SAN ANTONIO MISSIONS NATIONAL HISTORICAL PARK

The four missions preserved in San Antonio Missions National Historical Park are remnants of a massive system of colonization and cultural transformation established by Spain in the New World as early as the 16th century.

Missions were built along the San Antonio River starting in 1690 as outposts of both the Catholic Church and the Spanish government. These missions, staffed by Franciscan missionaries, were supported by the government because they helped support Spain's claims to these lands. French and British settlements were beginning to pop up in the southeast, encroaching on what Spain considered Spanish territory.

The missionaries' aim was to bring both Christianity and Spanish culture to Native Americans. They found some success among the small tribes, collectively known to the Spanish as the *Coahuiltecans,* who lived by hunting and gathering in eastern Texas and northern Mexico. These tribes were being pushed south by Apaches and north by Spanish colonization. Some of their number probably considered life inside the walls of the missions not entirely unappealing, especially as an alternative to starvation.

There were originally six missions established along the San Antonio River. The four that are preserved today, linked by a walking trail along the river in the heart of historic San Antonio, are Mission Concepción, Mission Espada, Mission San José, and Mission San Juan Capistrano. Another mission, San Antonio de Valero, is located at the trail's northern end; it is well known for its pivotal role in Texas history and is also called the Alamo.

The missions typically were fairly large compounds with high walls and gates for protection against raids by hostile tribes, such as the Apache. Inside the walls, the missions were designed to replicate Spanish culture, exposing the Native Americans to a completely foreign set of values, technologies, and skills. The theory was that this would ultimately not only convert the indigenous peoples to Christianity, but also turn them into a new kind of Spanish citizen.

In the late 1700s and early 1800s, the Spanish government began to withdraw its support for the mission system and the missions began to secularize. The four preserved in this national historical park, however, never fully secularized and still operate as Catholic parishes.

FRANK CHURCH RIVER OF NO RETURN WILDERNESS

I never knew a man who felt self-important in the morning after spending the night in the open on an Idaho mountainside under a star studded summer sky. Save some time in your lives for the outdoors, where you can be witness to the wonders of God.

—Frank Church

"A wilderness, in contrast with those areas where man and his own works dominate the landscape, is hereby recognized as an area where the earth and its community of life are untrammeled by man, where man himself is a visitor who does not remain." This definition comes from the Wilderness Act, signed in 1964 by President Lyndon Johnson. Since its approval, approximately nine million acres of land have been designated as wilderness.

The Frank Church River of No Return Wilderness is not named for a rancher, mountain man, or buckskin-clad explorer. Church showed courage and defied the odds in a different way: he was a four-term Democratic senator from Idaho. Church sponsored the Wilderness Act and, four years later, the Wild and Scenic Rivers Act. Just before leaving office, in 1980, he helped to create the River of No Return Wilderness, which was renamed in his honor shortly before his death in 1984. Fans of this sprawling reserve usually just call it "the Frank Church."

At 2.3 million acres, the Frank Church is the largest contiguous wilderness area in the continental United States. It is made up of mountains and canyonlands in six national forests in central Idaho. The "River of No Return" is the Salmon River, known for its whitewater rapids. "Picturesque" doesn't do justice to the wild beauty of the Salmon River canyonlands, the forested mountain slopes, and the snow-capped peaks found here.

Exploring and enjoying the Frank Church could occupy an outdoor adventurer's lifetime. There are 2,600 miles of Forest Service trails in the wilderness, and camping, big-game hunting, and fishing are all permitted. As the Forest Service's plan for this area puts it: "In so vast an area, opportunities for solitude abound and, in a general sense, evidence of man is substantially unnoticeable." This includes 20,000 acres of wilderness where the Forest Service maintains no trails.

FRANK CHURCH RIVER OF NO RETURN WILDERNESS

July 23, 1980 • U.S. Forestry Service

NATIONAL PARK OF AMERICAN SAMOA

If the National Parks System is a bridge between the known and the unknown, the National Park of American Samoa is the national park par excellence. Literally on the other side of the world, and abiding by a different set of laws and customs than the other parks, the National Park of American Samoa offers an invitation to explore an exciting, tropical world of volcanic mountains and coral reefs in the South Pacific.

American Samoa is made up a chain of seven volcanic islands. The park was established to preserve and protect the islands' natural resources, which include lush cloud forests, vibrant reefs, and pristine beaches. The National Park Service leases the land, rather than owning it outright, in keeping with local customs that prize families' traditional land holdings.

The park consists of 13,500 acres, including aquatic area, in three units located on three different islands. American Samoa's only international airport is located on the island of Tutuila, so this is the island that most visitors will see. One long trail takes hikers along the ridge of Mount Alava to its summit at 1,600 feet. From there the descent to Vatia, at the mountain's northern base, is fairly steep, requiring the use of ladders.

The park also includes 350 acres on Ofu island and 5,400 acres on Ta'u island, home of the park's cloud forest. A short plane ride takes visitors to these remote outposts of the park system.

Among the park's assets is the seclusion it offers. There are beaches and coral reefs around the world that attract tourists, but American Samoa is one of the most remote and undeveloped areas accessible to Americans without a passport. In 2005, National Park had fewer than 400 visitors.

Camping is not allowed in the park and there are few hotels on the island. In order to give visitors more options for lodging, the National Park Service has established a Home Stay program, which gives visitors a chance to stay with Samoan families. The National Park Service recommends that visitors who want to take advantage of this unique lodging alternative familiarize themselves with local customs prior to arriving.

WEIR FARM NATIONAL HISTORIC SITE

Weir and I would wander over that most picturesque if unprofitable pile of rocks he called his farm, and which he received from [a] Mr. Davis in exchange for a picture. Mr. Davis, judging by the rocks, thought he had the better of the artist, and Weir, judging by the inexhaustible beauty of woods, fields, hills, pond, granite boulders, and stone walls which he painted over and over again, knew that he had the better of the man of business.

—Augustus Vincent Tack, "A Letter"

Writing to a friend from his home in Connecticut in November 1902, painter J. Alden Weir expressed the importance of the land in his work, writing that it was his "hope and desire to get close to Nature, to know her character more intimately."

Weir was one of the Ten American Painters, sometimes called "The Ten." These artists, who generally were proponents of the Impressionist style, broke away from the Society of American Artists to protest what they believed was the Society's over-emphasis of commercial motives in the production of art. The Ten began holding their own exhibitions in the late 1890s, continuing for the next 20 years.

Weir bought the farm in Branchville, Connecticut, in 1882, five years after returning from the Ecole des Beaux-Arts in Paris. He built a studio on the property and used it as his summer home for 37 years. The farm's rolling hills and stone walls provided Weir with endless inspiration; he is said to have produced more than 250 paintings of this property.

Part of the value of this site lies in the fact that it preserves both Weir's studio and, to a large extent, his subject matter: the land. Few other parks in the nation give the visitor this kind of access into the "back room" life of a prominent American painter.

Guided tours of the buildings and grounds are available, as are self-guided tours of the "Painting Sites Trail," which is best hiked with the park's brochure in hand. The National Park Service hosts "Take Part in Art" on Wednesdays, Thursdays, and Fridays in the summer months. This free program lets visitors horn in on Alden's font of inspiration: the land. With sketching supplies on loan from the park, visitors can capture their impressions of the farm, creating their own souvenir and work of art.

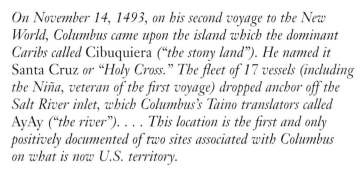

2020 · U.S. VIRGIN ISLANDS

SALT RIVER BAY NATIONAL HISTORICAL PARK AND ECOLOGICAL PRESERVE

On November 14, 1493, on his second voyage to the New World, Columbus came upon the island which the dominant Caribs called Cibuquiera *("the stony land"). He named it Santa Cruz or "Holy Cross." The fleet of 17 vessels (including the Niña, veteran of the first voyage) dropped anchor off the Salt River inlet, which Columbus's Taino translators called AyAy ("the river"). . . . This location is the first and only positively documented of two sites associated with Columbus on what is now U.S. territory.*

—National Park Service

The water in Salt River Bay on St. Croix is the alluring bright blue frequently found in the Caribbean. It beckons you to strap on a face mask and snorkel and dive in. Under the water, tropical fish are teeming around a coral reef and scuba divers are heading toward a canyon in the ocean's floor.

Back on land, there are more treasures to explore. Over the centuries since Europeans first discovered the Caribbean islands, several different powers have vied for control in the Virgin Islands, and they have left artifacts of their efforts all around this part of St. Croix.

When Columbus explored this area in his second voyage to the New World, in 1493, he sent armed men ashore to find fresh water and to look for inhabitants. The indigenous Caribs shot at them with arrows and Columbus's men retreated. This incident is believed to have taken place on the eastern shore of Salt River Bay, within the preserve's boundaries.

The Dutch, English, Spanish, French, and Danes all made efforts at establishing colonies here, beginning in the middle of the 17th century. When the Europeans were not being wiped out by one another, they were being devastated by tropical diseases or shifts in their fortunes. The most prominent remnants of the colonial era are the ruins of Fort Sale, a triangular earthwork fort originally built by the Dutch in the 1640s and later used by the various European powers attempting to control the islands.

Denmark owned the Virgin Islands from 1754 to 1917 and helped build the very lucrative sugar industry on the islands. The abolition of slavery in Danish colonies and the rise of the sugar beet in Europe both changed the Virgin Islands' fortunes once again, so much so that when the United States offered $25 million for the islands in 1917, the deal was accepted. Our nation's primary interest was to defend against the construction of a German submarine base in the islands during World War I.

MARSH-BILLINGS-ROCKEFELLER NATIONAL HISTORICAL PARK

Sight is a faculty, seeing an art. . . . [A]ctual observation of terrestrial surface affords to the eye the best general training that is accessible to all. . . . It may be profitably pursued by all, and every traveler, every lover of rural scenery, every agriculturist who will wisely use the gift of sight may add valuable contributions to the common stock of knowledge on a subject which, as I hope to convince my readers, . . . is not only a very important but a very interesting field of inquiry.

—**George S. Marsh, *Man and Nature***

George Perkins Marsh is widely regarded as America's first environmentalist. His book, *Man and Nature*, launched the modern conservation movement. "The operation of causes set in action by man," he said, "has brought the face of the earth to a desolation almost as complete as that of the moon." This statement might be considered controversial in some circles even today. Imagine how radical it was 150 years ago!

Marsh's status as a pioneering environmentalist makes it fitting that his childhood home near Woodstock, Vermont, is the centerpiece of a national historical park dedicated to the spirit of conservation. Something about the air of the place attracts dedicated environmentalists. The mansion, built in 1805, remained in the Marsh family until 1869, when it was purchased by Frederick Billings. Billings was a Vermont native who had gone west during the California Gold Rush. While there, he fell in love with the panoramic beauty of the area. *Man and Nature* was a call to action for him, and he became actively involved in advocating the creation of national parks at Yosemite and Yellowstone. After he purchased the Marsh homestead, he put his conservationist principles into action by reforesting much of the surrounding area.

The forest that Billings planted remains, and is probably the oldest managed forest in the United States. Hikers can enjoy the forest on 20 miles of carriage roads and trails, which link to the Appalachian National Scenic Trail about one mile from the park.

The park's continuing dedication to conservation is exemplified by its Forest Center, which was awarded the highest possible rating for Leadership in Environment and Energy Design by the United States Green Building Council. The building was constructed with Forest Stewardship Council–certified lumber from the park's own forest.

The park offers a walking tour, unique in the National Park System, that focuses on the civilian experience of the Civil War.

TALLGRASS PRAIRIE NATIONAL PRESERVE

Before plows broke the sod, much of the area between the Rocky Mountains and the Mississippi River was one huge blanket of prairie grasses. Some 400,000 square miles of the continent were prairie. Today, visitors to Tallgrass Prairie National Preserve get a sense of what it must have been like before this region became the nation's breadbasket.

Like the bison that grazed here, prairie grass used to be everywhere. The notion that the country could someday run out of it would have seemed absurd to early settlers. Over the past 150 years, partly as a result of this line of thinking, prairie has become increasingly rare. It is now plentiful only where conditions prevented successful planting of row crops.

The gently undulating limestone hills of eastern Kansas were too rocky to be good for agriculture, so this area was primarily used for grazing. Rancher Stephen Jones bought up 7,000 acres in the area and started raising cattle here in 1878. He had a mansion and a three-story barn built on the ranch using limestone quarried from the hills.

After Jones sold the property, it passed through several hands and was combined with other ranches. When it was sold to the Nature Conservancy in 2005, it was an 11,000-acre ranch, and had already been approved as part of the National Parks System. The land ownership at Tallgrass Reserve is unique: there are no long-term plans to turn the land over to public ownership. The reserve will be managed through a partnership between the Nature Conservancy and the National Park System.

Trails and self-guided tours offer visitors a chance to wade out into the "sea of grass" here, and to get a good look at the mansion and farm buildings on site. The nearly two-mile-long Southwide Nature Trail leads visitors to the historic one-room schoolhouse.

The park itself is still developing: its management plan calls for the introduction of bison herds in the future and for the restoration of the park's bottomland areas to prairie.

TALLGRASS PRAIRIE NATIONAL PRESERVE

TUSKEGEE AIRMEN NATIONAL HISTORIC SITE

Part of the function of the National Park System is to ensure that ordinary places where extraordinary things happened don't recede into the backdrop of the American landscape, where they might be swept aside at the whim of local or private interests.

Moton Field, a small municipal airport in rural Alabama, is one of these ordinary-looking places. But the short asphalt runway here leads ultimately to the streets of Selma and to the larger struggle for African American civil rights. During World War II this was the home of Tuskegee Army Air Field, training ground for the first African American fighter pilots.

Prior to the war, the U.S. armed forces were slow to promote African Americans to the level of officers. There were few African American officers in the late 1930s, and few African American troops were in combat positions. When Benjamin O. Davis Jr., the fourth black graduate in West Point's history, applied to the segregated Army Air Corps, he was rejected.

Davis was one of the first to sign up for training at Tuskegee Army Air Field when the program began in the summer of 1941. A year later, promoted to lieutenant colonel, he was the commander of the first all-black air unit, the 99th Fighter Squadron.

The 99th was assigned to North Africa in April 1943 and saw combat that June. As other all-black squadrons came out of Tuskegee, they joined the 99th and formed the 332nd Fighter Group. The 332nd flew 15,500 sorties and completed nearly 1,600 raids. To the crews of the bombers they defended, the Tuskegee Airmen became known as the "Red Tails," for the distinctive red marks on their planes, and as the "Red Tail Angels." They were highly respected and highly decorated. In 1945, the 332nd Fighter Group was presented with a Distinguished Unit Citation for its heroism.

The Tuskegee Airmen's superb performance obliterated the argument that blacks lacked the capacity to perform in combat at the same level as whites. This paved the way for integration of the armed forces, which was ordered by President Harry Truman three years after World War II. Benjamin O. Davis Jr. went on to become the first African American general in the U.S. Air Force.

Tuskegee Airmen National Historic Site at Moton Field is one of the most recent additions to the National Park System.

Step 1. The U.S. Mint initiated the site selection process by contacting the chief executive of each host jurisdiction (state, district, or territory) through a formal letter of request. The goal was to identify one preferred and three ranked alternative national sites in each jurisdiction. The Mint provided resources and access to lists of applicable national sites to each chief executive. National sites for consideration included any site under the supervision, management, or conservancy of the National Park Service, the U.S. Forest Service, the U.S. Fish and Wildlife Service, or any similar department or agency of the federal government.

Step 2. With due consideration to the requirement that the national site chosen for each host jurisdiction should be the most appropriate in terms of natural and historic significance, and after giving full and thoughtful consideration to national sites that are not under the jurisdiction of the secretary of the Interior, each chief executive provided the Mint his or her recommendation for the national site to be honored on the quarter, as well as three recommended alternative national sites in order of preference.

Step 3. The Mint reviewed all the recommendations and established a candidate list of the 56 national sites.

Step 4. The Mint consulted with the secretary of the Interior to ensure appropriateness of each of the 56 national site recommendations based on their natural or historic significance, and to validate the date on which each recommended site was established as a national site.

Step 5. Having consulted with each chief executive and with the secretary of the Interior, and having given full and thoughtful consideration to national sites that are not under the jurisdiction of the secretary of the Interior, the Mint reconciled all comments and recommended a final candidate list determined to be the most appropriate in terms of natural and historic significance to the secretary of the Treasury, who approved the final national site list. The approved list also established the order in which each quarter is released.

Appendix B
How the Coin Designs Were Selected

Step 1. The U.S. Mint initiated the formal design process for each national site as identified by the order of the official list approved by the secretary of the Treasury (see appendix A).

Step 2. The Mint contacted the head of the federal entity responsible for the supervision, management, or conservancy of each national site, asking him or her to appoint a knowledgeable federal official (e.g., national park superintendent, national forest supervisor, federal preservation officer) to serve as its liaison for the site. The liaison assisted the Mint by identifying source materials for candidate designs.

Step 3. Based on the source materials, the Mint produced three to five candidate designs focusing on aesthetic beauty, historical accuracy, authenticity, appropriateness, and coinability.

Step 4. The Mint consulted with the liaison for the federal entity responsible for the supervision, management, or conservancy of the national site to ensure the historical accuracy, authenticity, and overall composition of each candidate design to ensure it appropriately represents the site.

Step 5. Final candidate designs were submitted to the secretary of the Interior, the chief executive of the host jurisdiction (state, district, or territory), the Commission of Fine Arts (CFA), and the Citizens Coinage Advisory Committee (CCAC) for review and comment. Where necessary, the Mint made changes to address any concerns or recommendations resulting from this review process.

Step 6. The director of the Mint made a final recommendation to the secretary of the Treasury, after considering all relevant factors, including the comments and recommendations of the secretary of the Interior, the chief executive, the CFA, the CCAC, and the federal entity responsible for the supervision, management, or conservancy of each national site.

Step 7. The secretary of the Treasury made the final design selection.

In late 2009, the design-selection process for the 2010 quarter dollars was in its latter stages. Tentative designs had been submitted to the required groups and individuals (see step 5 in appendix B). The Commission of Fine Arts (CFA) had weighed in, and the Citizens Coinage Advisory Committee (CCAC) was scheduled to meet and compose its final recommendations.

The CFA noted that it would be an enormous challenge to depict sites as monumental in size as, say, Yellowstone National Park on a quarter dollar. It would be best, the CFA stated, to keep the designs simple and iconic, depicting the most well-known feature of each site. These were, in general, the CFA's guiding premises in making its design recommendations.

Of course, other parties had to review the designs and express their preferences before the secretary of the Treasury could make the final determination; the CFA was not the final arbiter of coin designs. The following pages examine the proposed 2010 designs from the point of view of these "insiders": their options, their recommendations, and the final selections for the first year of the new program.

HOT SPRINGS NATIONAL PARK

Four designs were submitted for Hot Springs National Park. All of the designs focused on the tangible structures of the famous bathhouses; designs 2, 3, and 4 included a suggestion of the mineral springs via the chalice-like fountain in front of the administration building.

The clearest and simplest of these, design number 2, was the CFA's recommendation. The design shows both the doorway of the park's main building, constructed during the Great Depression, and the fountain, centered in front of the door. (Design no. 3 shows both elements, but offset in a more complex layout; design no. 4 shows the fountain only.) Members of the commission were pleased with the design's simplicity (although, in general, they were less than pleased with the overall quality of the drawings).

Treasury Secretary's Final Choice: Design 2.

Design 1

Design 2

Design 3

Design 4

Hot Springs National Park, Arkansas

YELLOWSTONE NATIONAL PARK

The landscape of Yellowstone is complex and its features are massive, making it one of the most difficult national sites to capture on a tiny metal canvas. Thus, one of its simplest and most iconic features—the geyser known as Old Faithful—appears on all three proposed designs: with a bison in the foreground (design no. 1), with the Old Faithful Inn in the background (no. 2), and surrounded by trees and visitors (no. 3).

In the end, the CFA rejected all three designs, although was agreed that the focus should remain on the Old Faithful geyser. They recommended the paintings of Thomas Moran, among other resources, as guides for suitable designs.

Treasury Secretary's Final Choice: Design 1.

Yellowstone National Park, Wyoming

Design 1

Design 2

Design 3

YOSEMITE NATIONAL PARK

Like Yellowstone, Yosemite is among the largest and most striking landscapes in the United States, and thus presents some of the same difficulties. Yosemite Falls (the subject of designs 1 and 2), while recognizable in large photos, is less distinctive at half an inch tall. The same applies to the famous rock structure known as El Capitan (design no. 3), one of many features made famous by the photos of Ansel Adams.

Half Dome, however, is both simple and distinctive in shape; its sheer left face and curved right side are recognizable from other famous Adams photos, even to viewers who have never been to Yosemite. The CFA preferred the image of Half Dome in design number 4, but noted that the artwork seemed unfinished and suggested that other resources—like the famous Adams photographs—be studied to refine the image.

Treasury Secretary's Final Choice: Design 3.

Yosemite National Park, California

Design 1

Design 2

Design 3

Design 4

GRAND CANYON NATIONAL PARK

In addition to the sheer scale of the landscape, an added difficulty—as the CFA pointed out—is that the Grand Canyon was already featured on the Arizona quarter dollar in 2008. The new design not only had to be recognizable as the Grand Canyon, it had to be noticeably different from the statehood quarter's design.

Of the four proposed designs, the CFA preferred no. 1 because of the strong appearance of depth from foreground to background. The members suggested, however, that the loose rock (or "scree") in the foreground be deemphasized, and that the vertical edge of the cliff face that bisects the coin near the center be shifted to the right, to add even more depth to the composition.

Treasury Secretary's Final Choice: Design 1.

Grand Canyon National Park, Arizona

Design 1

Design 2

Design 3

Design 4

MT. HOOD NATIONAL FOREST

All four designs for the Mt. Hood National Forest quarter feature the outline of the mountain, centered, in the background, with varying elements between the mountain and the viewer—the Portland skyline; an orchard in the middleground; a forest at the base of the mountain; and the same forest, but with the addition of a wreath of flowers in the foreground.

As with the other designs, the CFA preferred the simplest, no. 3 (with forest and no flowers), for its "superior composition and simplicity of elements."

Treasury Secretary's Final Choice: Design 3.

Mount Hood National Park, Oregon

Design 1

Design 2

Design 3

Design 4

ALABAMA
- ❏ Horseshoe Bend National Military Park
- ❏ Little River Canyon National Preserve
- ❏ Russell Cave National Monument
- ❏ Selma to Montgomery National Historic Trail
- ❏ Tuskegee Airmen National Historic Site
- ❏ Tuskegee Institute National Historic Site

ALASKA
- ❏ Alagnak Wild River
- ❏ Alaska Public Lands
- ❏ Aleutian World War II National Historic Area
- ❏ Aniakchak National Monument and Preserve
- ❏ Bering Land Bridge National Preserve
- ❏ Cape Krusenstern National Monument
- ❏ Denali National Park and Preserve
- ❏ Gates of the Arctic National Park and Preserve
- ❏ Inupiat Heritage Center
- ❏ Katmai National Park and Preserve
- ❏ Kenai Fjords National Park
- ❏ Klondike Gold Rush National Historic Park
- ❏ Kobuk Valley National Park
- ❏ Lake Clark National Park and Preserve
- ❏ Noatak National Preserve
- ❏ Sitka National Historical Park
- ❏ Wrangell–Saint Elias National Park and Preserve
- ❏ Yukon–Charley Rivers National Preserve

AMERICAN SAMOA
- ❏ National Park of American Samoa

ARIZONA
- ❏ Canyon de Chelly National Monument
- ❏ Casa Grande Ruins National Monument
- ❏ Chiricahua National Monument
- ❏ Coronado National Memorial
- ❏ Fort Bowie National Historic Site
- ❏ Glen Canyon National Recreation Area
- ❏ Grand Canyon National Park
- ❏ Hohokam Pima National Monument
- ❏ Hubbell Trading Post National Historic Site
- ❏ Montezuma Castle National Monument
- ❏ Navajo National Monument
- ❏ Organ Pipe Cactus National Monument

- ❏ Petrified Forest National Park
- ❏ Pipe Spring National Monument
- ❏ Rainbow Bridge National Monument
- ❏ Saguaro National Park
- ❏ Sunset Crater Volcano National Monument
- ❏ Tonto National Monument
- ❏ Tumacácori National Historical Park
- ❏ Tuzigoot National Monument
- ❏ Walnut Canyon National Monument
- ❏ Wupatki National Monument
- ❏ Yuma Crossing National Heritage Area

ARKANSAS
- ❏ Arkansas Post National Memorial
- ❏ Buffalo National River
- ❏ Central High School National Historic Site
- ❏ Fort Smith National Historic Site
- ❏ Hot Springs National Park
- ❏ Pea Ridge National Military Park

CALIFORNIA
- ❏ Alcatraz Island
- ❏ Cabrillo National Monument
- ❏ Channel Islands National Park
- ❏ Death Valley National Park
- ❏ Devils Postpile National Monument
- ❏ Eugene O'Neill National Historic Site
- ❏ Fort Point National Historic Site
- ❏ Golden Gate National Recreation Area
- ❏ John Muir National Historic Site
- ❏ Joshua Tree National Park
- ❏ Juan Bautista de Anza National Historic Trail
- ❏ Kings Canyon National Park
- ❏ Lassen Volcanic National Park
- ❏ Lava Beds National Monument
- ❏ Manzanar National Historic Site
- ❏ Mojave National Preserve
- ❏ Muir Woods National Monument
- ❏ Pinnacles National Monument
- ❏ Point Reyes National Seashore
- ❏ Port Chicago Naval Magazine National Memorial
- ❏ Presidio of San Francisco
- ❏ Redwood National and State Parks
- ❏ Rosie the Riveter World War II Home Front National Historical Park
- ❏ San Francisco Maritime National Historical Park
- ❏ Santa Monica Mountains National Recreation Area
- ❏ Sequoia National Park
- ❏ Whiskeytown National Recreation Area
- ❏ Yosemite National Park

COLORADO
- ❏ Bent's Old Fort National Historic Site
- ❏ Black Canyon of the Gunnison National Park
- ❏ Cache la Poudre River Corridor
- ❏ Colorado National Monument
- ❏ Curecanti National Recreation Area
- ❏ Dinosaur National Monument
- ❏ Florissant Fossil Beds National Monument
- ❏ Great Sand Dunes National Park and Preserve

- ❏ Hovenweep National Monument
- ❏ Mesa Verde National Park
- ❏ Rocky Mountain National Park
- ❏ Sand Creek Massacre National Historic Site
- ❏ Yucca House National Monument

CONNECTICUT
- ❏ Quinebaug and Shetucket Rivers Valley National Heritage Corridor
- ❏ Weir Farm National Historic Site

DISTRICT OF COLUMBIA
- ❏ Anacostia Park
- ❏ Capitol Hill Parks
- ❏ Carter G. Woodson Home National Historic Site
- ❏ Civil War Defenses of Washington
- ❏ Constitution Gardens
- ❏ Ford's Theatre National Historic Site
- ❏ Fort Dupont Park
- ❏ Franklin Delano Roosevelt Memorial
- ❏ Frederick Douglass National Historic Site
- ❏ George Mason Memorial
- ❏ Harmony Hall
- ❏ John Ericsson National Memorial
- ❏ Kenilworth Park and Aquatic Gardens
- ❏ Korean War Veterans Memorial
- ❏ Lincoln Memorial
- ❏ Mary McLeod Bethune Council House National Historic Site
- ❏ Meridian Hill Park
- ❏ National Capital Parks–East
- ❏ National Mall and Memorial Parks
- ❏ National World War II Memorial
- ❏ Old Post Office Tower
- ❏ Peirce Mill
- ❏ Pennsylvania Avenue National Historic Site
- ❏ President's Park (White House)
- ❏ Rock Creek Park
- ❏ Sewall-Belmont House National Historic Site
- ❏ Suitland Parkway
- ❏ The Old Stone House
- ❏ Thomas Jefferson Memorial
- ❏ Vietnam Veterans Memorial
- ❏ Washington Monument
- ❏ World War II Memorial

FLORIDA
- ❏ Big Cypress National Preserve
- ❏ Biscayne National Park
- ❏ Canaveral National Seashore
- ❏ Castillo de San Marcos National Monument
- ❏ De Soto National Memorial
- ❏ Dry Tortugas National Park
- ❏ Everglades National Park
- ❏ Fort Caroline National Memorial
- ❏ Fort Matanzas National Monument
- ❏ Gulf Islands National Seashore
- ❏ Timucuan Ecological and Historic Preserve

GEORGIA
- ❏ Andersonville National Historic Site

- ❏ Augusta Canal National Heritage Area
- ❏ Chattahoochee River National Recreation Area
- ❏ Chickamauga and Chattahoochee National Military Park
- ❏ Cumberland Island National Seashore
- ❏ Fort Frederica National Monument
- ❏ Fort Pulaski National Monument
- ❏ Jimmy Carter National Historic Site
- ❏ Kennesaw Mountain National Battlefield Park
- ❏ Martin Luther King Jr. National Historic Site
- ❏ Ocmulgee National Monument

GUAM
- ❏ War in the Pacific National Historical Park

HAWAII
- ❏ Ala Kahakai National Historic Trail
- ❏ Haleakala National Park
- ❏ Hawai'i Volcanoes National Park
- ❏ Kalaupapa National Historical Park
- ❏ Kaloko-Honokohau National Historical Park
- ❏ Pu'uhonua O Honaunau National Historical Park
- ❏ Pu'ukohola Heiau National Historic Site
- ❏ World War II Valor in the Pacific National Monument

IDAHO
- ❏ City of Rocks National Reserve
- ❏ Craters of the Moon National Monument and Preserve
- ❏ Hagerman Fossil Beds National Monument
- ❏ Minidoka National Historic Site
- ❏ Nez Perce National Historical Park

ILLINOIS
- ❏ Lincoln Home National Historic Site

INDIANA
- ❏ George Rogers Clark National Historical Park
- ❏ Indiana Dunes National Lakeshore
- ❏ Lincoln Boyhood National Memorial

IOWA
- ❏ Effigy Mounds National Monument
- ❏ Herbert Hoover National Historic Site
- ❏ Silos and Smokestacks National Heritage Area

KANSAS
- ❏ Brown v. Board of Education National Historic Site
- ❏ Fort Larned National Historic Site
- ❏ Fort Scott National Historic Site
- ❏ Nicodemus National Historic Site
- ❏ Tallgrass Prairie National Preserve

KENTUCKY
- ❏ Abraham Lincoln Birthplace National Historic Site
- ❏ Cumberland Gap National Historical Park
- ❏ Mammoth Cave National Park

LOUISIANA
- ❏ Cane River National Heritage Area
- ❏ Cane River Creole National Historical Park
- ❏ Jean Lafitte National Historical Park and Preserve

❑ New Orleans Jazz National Historical Park
❑ Poverty Point National Monument

MAINE
❑ Acadia National Park
❑ Maine Acadian Culture
❑ Roosevelt Campobello National Park
❑ Saint Croix Island International Historic Site

MARYLAND
❑ Antietam National Battlefield
❑ Assateague Island National Seashore
❑ Baltimore-Washington Parkway
❑ Captain John Smith Chesapeake National Historic Trail
❑ Catoctin Mountain Park
❑ Chesapeake and Ohio Canal National Historical Park
❑ Chesapeake Bay Gateways Network
❑ Clara Barton National Historic Site
❑ Fort Foote Park
❑ Fort McHenry National Monument and Historic Shrine
❑ Fort Washington Park
❑ Glen Echo Park
❑ Greenbelt Park
❑ Hampton National Historic Site
❑ Monocacy National Battlefield
❑ Oxon Cove Park and Oxon Hill Farm
❑ Piscataway Park
❑ Star-Spangled Banner National Historic Trail
❑ Thomas Stone National Historic Site

MASSACHUSETTS
❑ Adams National Historical Park
❑ Boston National Historical Park
❑ Boston African American National Historic Site
❑ Boston Harbor Islands National Recreation Area
❑ Cape Cod National Seashore
❑ Essex National Heritage Area
❑ Frederick Law Olmstead National Historic Site
❑ John F. Kennedy National Historic Site
❑ Longfellow National Historic Site
❑ Lowell National Historical Park
❑ Minute Man National Historical Park
❑ New Bedford Whaling National Historical Park
❑ Salem Maritime National Historic Site
❑ Saugus Iron Works National Historic Site
❑ Springfield Armory National Historic Site

MICHIGAN
❑ Isle Royale National Park
❑ Keweenaw National Historical Park
❑ Motor Cities National Heritage Area
❑ Pictured Rocks National Lakeshore
❑ Sleeping Bear Dunes National Lakeshore

MINNESOTA
❑ Grand Portage National Monument
❑ Mississippi National River and Recreation Area
❑ Pipestone National Monument
❑ Voyageurs National Park

MISSISSIPPI
❑ Brices Cross Roads National Battlefield Site
❑ Natchez National Historical Park
❑ Natchez Trace Parkway
❑ Natchez Trace National Scenic Trail
❑ Tupelo National Battlefield
❑ Vicksburg National Military Park

MISSOURI
❑ George Washington Carver National Monument
❑ Harry S. Truman National Historic Site
❑ Jefferson National Expansion Memorial
❑ Ozark National Scenic Riverways
❑ Ulysses S. Grant National Historic Site
❑ Wilson's Creek National Battlefield

MONTANA
❑ Big Hole National Battlefield
❑ Bighorn Canyon National Recreation Area
❑ Glacier National Park
❑ Grant-Kohrs Ranch National Historic Site
❑ Little Bighorn Battlefield National Monument

NEBRASKA
❑ Agate Fossil Beds National Monument
❑ Homestead National Monument of America
❑ Lewis and Clark National Historic Trail
❑ Missouri National Recreational River
❑ Niobrara National Scenic River
❑ Scotts Bluff National Monument

NEVADA
❑ Great Basin National Park
❑ Lake Mead National Recreation Area

NEW HAMPSHIRE
❑ Saint-Gaudens National Historic Site

NEW JERSEY
❑ Edison National Historic Site
❑ Morristown National Historical Park
❑ New Jersey Coastal Heritage Trail Route
❑ New Jersey Pinelands National Reserve

NEW MEXICO
❑ Aztec Ruins National Monument
❑ Bandelier National Monument
❑ Capulin Volcano National Monument
❑ Carlsbad Caverns National Park
❑ Chaco Culture National Historical Park
❑ El Camino Real de los Tejas National Historic Trail
❑ El Camino Real de Tierra Adentro National Historic Trail
❑ El Malpais National Monument
❑ El Morro National Monument
❑ Fort Union National Monument
❑ Gila Cliff Dwellings National Monument
❑ Northern Rio Grande National Heritage Area
❑ Old Spanish National Historic Trail
❑ Pecos National Historical Park
❑ Petroglyph National Monument
❑ Salinas Pueblo Missions National Monument

- Santa Fe National Historic Trail
- Trail of Tears National Historic Trail
- White Sands National Monument

NEW YORK
- African Burial Ground National Monument
- Castle Clinton National Monument
- Eleanor Roosevelt National Historic Site
- Ellis Island National Monument
- Erie Canalway National Heritage Corridor
- Federal Hall National Memorial
- Fire Island National Seashore
- Fort Stanwix National Monument
- Gateway National Recreation Area
- General Grant National Memorial
- Governors Island National Monument
- Hamilton Grange National Memorial
- Home of Franklin D. Roosevelt National Historic Site
- Hudson River Valley National Heritage Area
- Lower East Side Tenement Museum National Historic Site
- Manhattan Sites
- Martin Van Buren National Historic Site
- National Parks of New York Harbor
- Niagara Falls National Heritage Area
- Sagamore Hill National Historic Site
- Saint Paul's Church National Historic Site
- Saratoga National Historical Park
- Statue of Liberty National Monument
- Theodore Roosevelt Birthplace National Historic Site
- Theodore Roosevelt Inaugural National Historic Site
- Vanderbilt Mansion National Historic Site
- Women's Rights National Historical Park

NORTH CAROLINA
- Blue Ridge Parkway
- Blue Ridge National Heritage Area
- Cape Hatteras National Seashore
- Cape Lookout National Seashore
- Carl Sandberg Home National Historic Site
- Fort Raleigh National Historic Site
- Guilford Courthouse National Military Park
- Moores Creek National Battlefield
- Wright Brothers National Memorial

NORTH DAKOTA
- Fort Union Trading Post National Historic Site
- Knife River Indian Villages National Historic Site
- Theodore Roosevelt National Park

NORTHERN MARIANA ISLANDS
- American Memorial Park

OHIO
- Cuyahoga Valley National Park
- David Berger National Memorial
- Dayton Aviation Heritage National Historical Park
- First Ladies National Historic Site

- Hopewell Culture National Historical Park
- James A. Garfield National Historic Site
- National Aviation Heritage Area
- Perry's Victory and International Peace Memorial
- William Howard Taft National Historic Site

OKLAHOMA
- Chickasaw National Recreation Area
- Oklahoma City National Memorial
- Washita Battlefield National Historic Site

OREGON
- Crater Lake National Park
- John Day Fossil Beds National Monument
- Lewis and Clark National Historical Park
- Oregon Caves National Monument

PENNSYLVANIA
- Allegheny Portage Railroad National Historic Site
- Delaware National Scenic River
- Delaware and Lehigh National Heritage Corridor
- Delaware Water Gap National Recreation Area
- Deshler-Morris House
- Edgar Allan Poe National Historic Site
- Eisenhower National Historic Site
- Flight 93 National Memorial
- Fort Necessity National Battlefield
- Friendship Hill National Historic Site
- Gettysburg National Military Park
- Gloria Dei Church National Historic Site
- Great Egg Harbor River
- Hopewell Furnace National Historic Site
- Independence National Historic Park
- Johnstown Flood National Memorial
- Lackawanna Heritage Valley
- Lower Delaware National Wild and Scenic River
- Oil Region National Heritage Area
- Path of Progress National Heritage Tour Route
- Rivers of Steel National Heritage Area
- Schuylkill River Valley National Heritage Area
- Steamtown National Historic Site
- Thaddeus Kosciuszko National Memorial
- Upper Delaware Scenic and Recreational River
- Valley Forge National Historical Park

PUERTO RICO
- San Juan National Historic Site

RHODE ISLAND
- Blackstone River Valley National Heritage Corridor
- Roger Williams National Memorial
- Touro Synagogue National Historic Site

SOUTH CAROLINA
- Charles Pinckney National Historic Site
- Congaree National Park
- Cowpens National Battlefield
- Fort Sumter National Monument
- Gullah/Geechee Cultural Heritage Corridor
- Kings Mountain National Military Park
- Ninety Six National Historic Site

- ❏ Overmountain Victory National Historic Trail
- ❏ South Carolina National Heritage Corridor

SOUTH DAKOTA
- ❏ Badlands National Park
- ❏ Jewel Cave National Monument
- ❏ Minuteman Missile National Historic Site
- ❏ Mount Rushmore National Memorial
- ❏ Wind Cave National Park

TENNESSEE
- ❏ Andrew Johnson National Historic Site
- ❏ Big South Fork National River and Recreation Area
- ❏ Fort Donelson National Battlefield
- ❏ Great Smoky Mountains National Park
- ❏ Obed Wild and Scenic River
- ❏ Shiloh National Military Park
- ❏ Stones River National Battlefield
- ❏ Tennessee Civil War National Heritage Area

TEXAS
- ❏ Amistad National Recreation Area
- ❏ Big Bend National Park
- ❏ Big Thicket National Preserve
- ❏ Chamizal National Memorial
- ❏ Fort Davis National Historic Site
- ❏ Guadalupe Mountains National Park
- ❏ Lake Meredith National Recreation Area
- ❏ Lyndon B. Johnson National Historical Park
- ❏ Padre Island National Seashore
- ❏ Palo Alto Battlefield National Historical Park
- ❏ Rio Grande Wild and Scenic River
- ❏ San Antonio Missions National Historical Park

UTAH
- ❏ Arches National Park
- ❏ Bryce Canyon National Park
- ❏ California National Historic Trail
- ❏ Canyonlands National Park
- ❏ Capitol Reef National Park
- ❏ Cedar Breaks National Monument
- ❏ Golden Spike National Historic Site
- ❏ Mormon Pioneer National Historic Trail
- ❏ Natural Bridges National Monument
- ❏ Oregon National Historic Trail
- ❏ Parashant National Monument
- ❏ Pony Express National Historic Trail
- ❏ Timpanogos Cave National Monument
- ❏ Zion National Park

VERMONT
- ❏ Marsh-Billings-Rockefeller National Historical Park

VIRGIN ISLANDS
- ❏ Buck Island Reef National Monument
- ❏ Christiansted National Historic Site
- ❏ Salt River Bay National Historic Park and Ecological Preserve
- ❏ Virgin Islands National Park
- ❏ Virgin Islands Coral Reef National Monument

VIRGINIA
- ❏ Appomattox Court House National Historical Park
- ❏ Arlington House: The Robert E. Lee Memorial
- ❏ Booker T. Washington National Monument
- ❏ Cape Henry Memorial
- ❏ Cedar Creek and Belle Grove National Historical Park
- ❏ Claude Moore Colonial Farm
- ❏ Colonial National Historical Park
- ❏ Fredericksburg and Spotsylvania National Military Park
- ❏ George Washington Memorial Parkway
- ❏ George Washington Birthplace National Monument
- ❏ Great Falls Park
- ❏ Green Springs
- ❏ Jamestown National Historic Site
- ❏ Lyndon Baines Johnson Memorial Grove on the Potomac
- ❏ Maggie L. Walker National Historic Site
- ❏ Manassas National Battlefield Park
- ❏ Petersburg National Battlefield
- ❏ Prince William Forest Park
- ❏ Richmond National Battlefield Park
- ❏ Shenandoah National Park
- ❏ Theodore Roosevelt Island Park
- ❏ Wolf Trap National Park for the Performing Arts
- ❏ Yorktown National Cemetery

WASHINGTON
- ❏ Ebey's Landing National Historical Reserve
- ❏ Fort Vancouver National Historic Site
- ❏ Klondike Gold Rush–Seattle Unit National Historical Park
- ❏ Lake Chelan National Recreation Area
- ❏ Lake Roosevelt National Recreation Area
- ❏ Mount Rainier National Park
- ❏ North Cascades National Park
- ❏ Olympic National Park
- ❏ Ross Lake National Recreation Area
- ❏ San Juan Island National Historical Park
- ❏ Whitman Mission National Historic Site

WEST VIRGINIA
- ❏ Appalachian National Scenic Trail
- ❏ Bluestone National Scenic River
- ❏ Gauley River National Recreation Area
- ❏ Harpers Ferry National Historical Park
- ❏ New River Gorge National River
- ❏ Potomac Heritage National Scenic Trail
- ❏ Wheeling National Heritage Area

WISCONSIN
- ❏ Apostle Islands National Lakeshore
- ❏ Ice Age National Scenic Trail
- ❏ North Country National Scenic Trail
- ❏ Saint Croix National Scenic River

WYOMING
- ❏ Devils Tower National Monument
- ❏ Fort Laramie National Historic Site
- ❏ Fossil Butte National Monument
- ❏ Grand Teton National Park
- ❏ John D. Rockefeller Jr. Memorial Parkway
- ❏ Yellowstone National Park

By park:

About the Author

Growing up a stone's throw from the Adirondack Mountains, author **Aaron J. McKeon** learned the simple pleasures of a good hike at an early age. As a freelance writer and a member of the American Institute of Certified  Planners, McKeon focuses his work on innovative ways to strike a balance between the demands of the man-made world and the preservation of natural resources. He lives in Syracuse, New York, where he and his wonderful wife, Courtenay, sometimes manage to keep up with their two boys.

Illustration Credits